Biography

James Egan was born in 1985 and grew up in
Portarlington, Co. Laois in the Midlands of Ireland.
In 2008, James moved to England and studied in Oxford.
James married his wife in 2012 and currently lives in
Havant in Hampshire.
James had his first book, 365 Ways to Stop Sabotaging
Your Life, published in 2014.
Several of James' books have become No.1 Best Sellers
in the UK including 1000 Facts about Horror Movies,
3000 Facts About the Greatest Movies Ever, 365 Things
People Believe That Aren't True, Another 365 Things
People Believe That Aren't True, and 500 Things People
Believe That Aren't True.

Books by James Egan

Fairytale
Inherit the Earth
Hilarious Things That Kids Say
Hilarious Things That Mums Say
3000 Facts about TV Shows
3000 Facts about Animated Shows
3000 Facts about Actors
3000 Facts about Countries
Dinosaurs Had Feathers (and other Random Facts)
3000 Facts about Animals
1000 Facts about James Bond
1000 Inspiring Facts
The Pocketbook of Phobias
How to Psychologically Survive Cancer
1000 Out-of-this-World Facts about Space
3000 Facts about the Greatest Movies Ever
1000 Facts about Film Directors
1000 Facts about Superhero Movies
1000 Facts about Superheroes Vol. 1-3
1000 Facts about Supervillains Vol. 1-3
1000 Facts about Comic Books
3000 Facts about Animated Films
1000 Facts about Horror Movies
1000 Facts about American Presidents
Adorable Animal Facts
3000 Facts about Video Games
500 Things People Believe That Aren't True
1000 Things People Believe That Aren't True
3000 Astounding Quotes
1000 Facts About Comic Book Characters Vol. 1-3
100 Classic Stories in 100 Pages
Words That Need to Exist in English
500 Facts about Godzilla
365 Ways to Stop Sabotaging Your Life

1000 Facts about Writers

by

James Egan

Copyright 2016 © James Egan

All rights reserved. No part of this book may be reproduced, stored, or transmitted by any means - whether auditory, graphic, mechanical, or electronic - without written permission of both publisher and author, except in the case of brief excerpts used in critical articles and reviews. Unauthorised reproduction of any part of this work is illegal. Unauthorised reproduction of any part of this work is illegal and is punishable by law.

ISBN: 978-0-244-93009-7

Because of the dynamic nature of the Internet, any web addresses or links contain in this book may have changed since publication and may no longer be valid. The views expressed in this work are solely those of the author and do not necessarily reflect the views of the publisher, and the publisher hereby disclaims any responsibility for them.

Any people depicted in stock imagery provided by Thinkstock are models, and such images are being used for illustrative purposes only.
Certain stock imagery © Thinkstock.

Lulu Publishing Services rev. date: 11/09/2017

*Dedicated to
Shannon "Headtap" Thorncroft*

Content

1. Aeschylus		p9
2. Agatha Christie		p11
3. Aldous Huxley		p13
4. Alexandre Dumas		p15
5. Anne Frank		p17
6. Anne Rice		p19
7. Anton Chekov		p21
8. Arthur Conan Doyle		p23
9. Arthur Miller		p25
10.	Ayn Rand	p28
11.	Beatrix Potter	p30
12.	Ben Jonson	p32
13.	Brothers Grimm	p34
14.	Bram Stoker	p36
15.	CS Lewis	p38
16.	Charles Dickens	p40
17.	Charlotte Bronte	p43
18.	Christopher Marlowe	p45
19.	Chuck Palahniuk	p47
20.	Cormac McCarthy	p49
21.	Daniel Defoe	p51
22.	Dante Alighieri	p53
23.	Douglas Adams	p55
24.	Dr. Seuss	p57
25.	Edgar Allen Poe	p59
26.	Edgar Rice Burroughs	p61
27.	Emily Bronte	p63
28.	Emily Dickinson	p65
29.	Ernest Hemingway	p67
30.	F. Scott Fitzgerald	p69
31.	Frank Herbert	p71
32.	Franz Kafka	p73
33.	Fyodor Dostoevsky	p75
34.	Geoffrey Chaucer	p77

35.	George Bernard Shaw	p79
36.	George Orwell	p80
37.	George RR Martin	p82
38.	HG Wells	p84
39.	HP Lovecraft	p86
40.	Hans Christian Andersen	p88
41.	Harper Lee	p90
42.	Herman Melville	p92
43.	Homer	p94
44.	Hunter S. Thompson	p96
45.	Isaac Asimov	p99
46.	JD Salinger	p101
47.	JK Rowling	p103
48.	JM Barrie	p105
49.	JRR Tolkien	p107
50.	James Joyce	p109
51.	Jane Austen	p111
52.	Jean Paul Sartre	p113
53.	Johann Wolfgang von Goethe	p114
54.	John Milton	p116
55.	John Steinbeck	p118
56.	Jonathan Swift	p120
57.	Joseph Conrad	p122
58.	Jules Verne	p124
59.	Kenneth Grahame	p126
60.	Kurt Vonnegut	p128
61.	L. Frank Baum	p130
62.	Leo Tolstoy	p132
63.	Lewis Carroll	p134
64.	Lord Byron	p136
65.	Louisa May Alcott	p138
66.	Mark Twain	p140
67.	Mary Shelley	p142
68.	Maya Angelou	p144
69.	Michael Crichton	p146
70.	Miguel de Cervantes	p148
71.	Miscellaneous	p150

72.	Nathaniel Hawthorne	p152
73.	Oscar Wilde	p154
74.	Philip K. Dick	p156
75.	RL Stine	p158
76.	Ray Bradbury	p159
77.	Raymond Chandler	p161
78.	Roald Dahl	p163
79.	Robert Frost	p165
80.	Robert Louis Stevenson	p167
81.	Rudyard Kipling	p168
82.	Salman Rushdie	p170
83.	Samuel Beckett	p172
84.	Sophocles	p174
85.	Stephen King	p176
86.	Sylvia Plath	p178
87.	TS Eliot	p180
88.	Tennessee Williams	p182
89.	Terry Pratchett	p184
90.	Tom Clancy	p186
91.	Toni Morrison	p188
92.	Truman Capote	p190
93.	Victor Hugo	p192
94.	Virginia Woolf	p194
95.	Vladimir Nabokov	p196
96.	Voltaire	p198
97.	William S. Burroughs	p199
98.	William Butler Yeats	p201
99.	William Golding	p203
100.	William Shakespeare	p204

Aeschylus

525 BC – 456 BC

Written Work
The Persians (472 BC)
Seven Against Thebes (467 BC)
The Oresteia (458 BC)

1. Aeschylus is the founder of Ancient Greek drama. He is known as the Father of Tragedy.

2. He was the first playwright who clad his actors in costumes when they performed plays.

3. Aeschylus was born in Eleusis in Greece. Eleusis is situated several miles from Athens.

4. Although Aeschylus wrote up to 90 plays, only seven of them have survived – The Persians, Seven Against Thebes, The Suppliants, The Oresteia Trilogy (composed of Agamemnon, The Libation Bearers, and The Eumenides,) and Prometheus Bound. However, some historians are uncertain as to whether Aeschylus wrote Prometheus Bound since Zeus is depicted as a tyrant in the story while he is perceived as a noble ruler in Aeschylus' previous plays.

5. The Persians is the only Ancient Greek drama not based on myth. It was also the first Ancient Greek drama that revolved around modern history since the Battle of Salamis was part of the story. This battle only took place eight years before the play was performed. Aeschylus fought in Salamis and personally battled against the forces of Xerxes. Xerxes infamously battled Leonidas of Sparta.

6. One of his most famous quotes is, "In war, truth is the first casualty."

7. He was a member of a cult called The Eleusian Mysteries. Members of this group believed that they gained sacred knowledge if they worshipped the Goddess of Agriculture, Demeter.

8. He had two sons called Euphorion and Euaeon. Both of them grew up to be writers of tragic poems. Euphorian's poetry was so good, he beat Sophocles and Euripides in poetry competitions. Sophocles and Euripides were among the greatest storytellers of Ancient Greece.

9. His lost plays include The Argo, Children of Hercules, Circe, Daughters of Helios, Philoctetes, The Sphinx, and Prometheus the Fire-Bearer. Other lost plays including The Myrmidons, Nereids, Hector's Ransom, and Niobe were based on chapters of Homer's The Iliad.

10. Allegedly, a fortune-teller told Aeschylus that he would be struck dead by a blow from the Heavens. Shortly after, he was killed when an eagle dropped a tortoise on his head. The man knew how to make an exit.

Agatha Christie

1890 – 1976

Written Work
Poirot series (1920-1975)
Miss Marple series (1932-1976)
The Mousetrap (1952)

11. The most iconic character in Agatha Christie's work is the Belgian detective, Hercule Poirot. He has appeared in 33 novels and over 50 short stories. He was played by David Suchet for 34 years in the TV series, Poirot.

    Ironically, Christie thought the character was "insufferable" and a "detestable, bombastic, tiresome ego-centric little creep." The only reason she didn't kill him off was because she made most of her money from his stories.

12. Christie has sold two billion copies of her work, which is more than any other writer apart from Shakespeare. Her most successful novel, And Then There Were None, has sold over 100 million copies. It is the seventh most successful novel ever written.

13. She married Archibald Christie in 1914. She was very unhappy in the marriage and disappeared in 1926. But Agatha Christie didn't just leave Archibald. She vanished. She wasn't found for ten days and she could never explain where she was. This was a media sensation and made front-page news. A 2006 biographer considered that Christie was under so much stress in her failed marriage, it gave her amnesia during this time

14. Christie loved archaeology and met her second husband, Max Mallowan at an excavation site. She married him in 1930 and they remained happily married until Christie's death in 1976.

15. She didn't smoke or drink. Weirdly, Christie tried to smoke for six months but didn't like the taste.

16. She wrote six novels under the pseudonym, Mary Westmacott. Christie wrote Absent in the Spring under this name. She wrote the book in a single weekend.

17. She wrote 66 novels and 14 short story collections.

18. The character, Miss Marple, appeared in 12 crime novels and 20 short stories. She is a spinster who acts like an amateur detective. She is based on Christie's grandmother.

19. She wrote the murder mystery play, The Mousetrap, that began its run in London's West End on October 6th 1952. It has been running for over 60 years, making it the longest running play ever. The show had its 25,000th performance on November 18th 2012.

20. Her novel, The Pale Horse, describes thallium poisoning so meticulously, a nurse reading the book was able to diagnose a toddler that left doctors baffled. This means that Agatha Christie saved a child's life a year after the writer died.

Aldous Huxley

1894 – 1963

Written Work
Brave New World (1932)
Island (1962)
Point Counter Point (1928)

21. Aldous Leonard Huxley studied at Eton College in Berkshire, England, and eventually became a teacher there. When George Orwell was a student at Eton, he was taught French by Huxley. Orwell went on to write Animal Farm and Nineteen Eighty-Four. Although Huxley is best known for his novel, Brave New World, Orwell believed that the story was plagiarised from a 1923 novel called We. In 1949, Huxley wrote a letter to Orwell, praising him for Nineteen Eighty-Four but said that Brave New World provided a more accurate picture of the future.

22. Huxley wrote a screenplay for the Disney version of Alice in Wonderland. It was rejected since he used convoluted language which children wouldn't understand. The hookah-smoking caterpillar is a nod to Huxley's smoking habit.

23. He wrote 11 novels, nine screenplays, six short story collections, and nine poem collections.

24. Huxley had a tragic childhood. His mother died of cancer, his brother took his own life, and Huxley nearly went blind as a teenage due to inflamed corneas. Although his sight improved, he struggled with his vision for the rest of his life.

25. He wrote for Vanity Fair and Vogue.

26. His father, Thomas Huxley, was a biologist and passionately defended Charles Darwin's Survival of the Fittest Theory. He defended evolution so often, he got the nickname, Darwin's Bulldog.

    Also, Thomas Huxley coined the word "agnostic."

27. Huxley was fascinated by parapsychology and philosophical mysticism.

28. The musician, Jim Morrison, named his band, The Doors, as a reference to Huxley's novel, The Doors of Perception.

29. Huxley was passionately vocal about his distaste for drugs, believing that they numbed emotions. Weirdly, he took LSD, assuming it was harmless. While Huxley was on his deathbed, he wrote out a request for LSD to numb his pain.

30. His 1932 book, Brave New World, looks at a disturbing future for humanity. The story takes place in 2540, where humanity has become reliant on drugs that repress anxiety. This book was written at least 20 years before clinical trials for antidepressants were carried out. In this future, babies are born in test tubes instead of through natural means. Huxley wrote about this concept 46 years before the first test-tube baby became a reality.

Alexandre Dumas

1802 – 1870

Written Work
The Three Musketeers (1844)
The Count of Monte Cristo (1844-1846)

31. His real name was Dumas Davy de la Pailleterie.

32. Dumas is one of the most influential French writers of all time. His work has been translated into almost 100 languages. His published works total 100,000 pages. There have been nearly 200 film adaptions of his works, mainly The Three Musketeers.

33. The historian, George Saintsbury, stated that The Count of Monte Cristo was the most popular book in Europe for several years.

34. The Count of Monte Cristo revolves around a man called Dantes who is falsely imprisoned by his jealous friend, Mondego. Dantes escapes and vows to destroy Mondego's life. The story was first printed in 18 segments in the French newspaper, Journal de debats. The first section was printed in the paper on August 28th 1844. The story concluded on January 15th 1846.

35. His father, Thomas–Alexandre, was African-American. He was the highest-ranking person of colour in the Continental European army.

36. Originally, The Count of Monte Cristo was misspelt as The Count of Monte Christo.

37. Although Dumas never officially declared that the characters in The Count of Monte Cristo, Eugenie

Danglars and Louise d'Armilly, were involved in a homosexual relationship, there was enough implication for some of their sections to be removed. These sections weren't available in English for 150 years.

38. Dumas was an expert fencer. By the time he was 10, he was such a skilled swordsman, he duelled with adults.

39. The Three Musketeers are Athos, Porthos and Aramis. They were based on real musketeers. The lead character, D'Artagnan, was based on Captain Charles de Batz-Castelmore, who served Louis VIV. He died at the Siege of Masstricht in the Franco-Dutch War.

40. Nobody knows who translated The Count of Monte Cristo into English. However, one unofficial English version was translated by Emma Lavinia Gifford. She was married to writer, Thomas Hardy, who wrote Return of the Native, Far from the Madding Crowd, and The Mayor of Casterbridge.

Anne Frank

1929 – 1945

Written Work
The Diary of a Young Girl (1947)

41. Annelies Marie Frank was born in Frankfurt, Germany, to Jewish parents, Otto and Edith Frank. Her family emigrated to the Netherlands when Anne Frank was four years old due to the stigma that Jewish people had in Germany. When the Nazis invaded the Netherlands, her family went into hiding.

42. She hid in several concealed rooms behind a bookcase in the building where her father worked. Eight other people lived with Anne Frank during this time. It is here that she wrote her diary.

43. Eleanor Roosevelt provided the introduction for her book.

44. Some people believe that Anne Frank's diary is a fake, stating that a 13-year-old girl couldn't write such a polished book. Academic studies have been performed on the diary and they confirmed it was irrefutably written by Anne Frank.

45. She started writing her diary on her 13th birthday. It was written between 1942 and 1944 and was published in 1947.

46. Anne Frank wrote two diaries. Nowadays, they are simply known as A and B. A was the original and B was a rewrite. Her father edited A and B to depict his daughter in the best way. For example, B left out a passage where Anne talked about a birthday. By the

time she wrote B, she was older and thought this section sounded too childish. Otto reinserted this part in the finalized book as it depicted his daughter as innocent and passionate.

He also reinserted passages from A that made him appear as a role model and reinserted passages that depicted Anne's mother and his wife in a negative light.

47. Otto tore out five pages of the diaries. These pages were not publicly revealed until the 1990s. In those pages, Anne Frank wrote that the diary shouldn't be read by her family as it's "none of their business."

48. Anne Frank was only 15 when she died in a concentration camp. It is believed she died from typhoid.

49. She dreamed of being a journalist.

50. Otto Frank was the only member of her family to survive World War II. It was he who saved her diary. If it wasn't for him, nobody would've ever read The Diary of a Young Girl.

Anne Rice

1941 -

Written Work
Interview with the Vampire (1976)
Queen of the Damned (1988)

51. Her real name is Howard O' Brien. Her mother named her Howard believing this would give her an advantage in life... somehow.

52. Anne Rice is best known for writing The Vampire Chronicles, which revolves around the vampire, Lestat. The Vampire Chronicles are made up of Interview with the Vampire, The Vampire Lestat, The Queen of the Damned, Tale of the Body Thief, Memnoch the Devil, The Vampire Armand, Merrick, Blood and Gold, Blackwood Farm, Blood Canticle, and Prince Lestat.

53. Interview with the Vampire was adapted into a film in 1994. When Rice wrote the book in 1976, she pictured Rutger Hauer playing the role. By the time the film was in production, Hauer was too old for the role and the part was offered to Jeremy Irons. After he turned it down, Tom Cruise was cast as Lestat. Rice was outraged saying the casting was "so bizarre; it's almost impossible to imagine how it's going to work" and it was "the worst crime in the name of casting since The Bonfire of the Vanities." Although she refused to watch the film, the producer sent a copy. She was blown away by Cruise's performance and sent him an apology.

54. She married Stan Rice when she was 20 and he was 19. They had a daughter called Michele and a son called Christopher. Michelle died from leukaemia when she was only six years old.

55. Her son wrote many best-selling novels including A Density of Souls, The Snow Garden, and The Vines.

56. Anne Rice has sold over 100 million copies of her work.

57. She wrote erotic novels under several pseudonyms.

58. Rice became a born-again Christian in 1998. Although she abandoned Christianity in 2010, she still claims to be religious. She wrote three books about Jesus Christ called the Christ the Lord trilogy. They are made up of Out of Egypt, The Road to Cana, and The Kingdom of Heaven.

59. She has written over 30 novels.

60. Anne Rice is a great author and is directly responsible for popularising vampire lore during the 1990s…but there's one thing she is not good at - dealing with criticism. When Amazon customers give her books bad reviews, she replied to their comments by accusing them of "slander" and said they were using the website as "a public urinal to publish falsehood and lies." Also, Rice doesn't retaliate with one or two comments. One of her replies is 1,200 words long!

Anton Chekhov

1860 – 1904

Written Work
Three Sisters (1901)
The Seagull (1896)
Ivanov (1903)
The Cherry Orchard (1903)
Uncle Vanya (1887)

61. Anton Pavlovich Chekhov was a Russian playwright and is considered to be one of the most influential writers ever. However, he saw himself as a doctor rather than a playwright. He stated that "literature is my mistress" while "medicine was my lawful wife." He charged nothing when he treated the poor.

62. One of his pseudonyms was Man Without A Spleen.

63. Although The Seagull is one of his greatest plays, it received poor reviews when it premiered in 1896. Chekhov was so devastated, that he renounced theatre. When Konstantin Stanislavski put the play on in the Moscow Art Theatre two years later, it became a massive success and Chekhov returned to writing.

64. Originally, Chekhov wrote stories simply to make money. As he became successful, Chekhov's ambition grew and he wished to write more complex stories to make the readers think. Chekhov thought it was an artist's duty to ask questions in his work, not answer them. His short story, The Lady with the Dog, is considered by many to be the greatest short story ever written.

65. He married an actress called Olga Knipper in 1901.

66. Henry Ibsen, August Strindberg, and Anton Chekhov are the three figures who are responsible for birthing early modernism in theatre. Modernism is a philosophy that details how trends changed in Western society in the late 19th and early 20th century due to the growth of industrial societies.

67. His mother entertained Chekhov with stories during his childhood. His father, however, was an abusive man and inspired many antagonistic characters in Chekhov's work.

68. Near the end of his life, Chekhov was the most famous Russian writer apart from Leo Tolstoy.

69. He was only 44 when he died of tuberculosis. He was buried beside his father.

70. His nephew was Michael Chekhov. He was an actor who was taught by Konstanin Stanislavski, who is considered to be the greatest acting teacher in Russian history. Michael Chekhov became an astounding actor and Stanislavski referred to him as his greatest student. Michael Chekhov's book, Into the Actor, details all his acting techniques and is regarded as one of the most influential acting books ever. His techniques have been used by actors like Marilyn Monroe, Clint Eastwood, and Jack Nicholson.

Arthur Conan Doyle

1859 – 1930

Written Work
Sherlock Holmes series (1888-1914)
The Lost World (1912)

71. Sir Arthur Ignatius Conan Doyle was a British writer who specialised in detective fiction. Originally, he was a physician.

72. His story, The Lost World, revolves around a newly discovered land populated by prehistoric monsters and dinosaurs. It was adapted into a film in 1925 and was the first film to be shown on an airplane. Although the 1933 classic, King Kong, popularised stop-motion, The Lost World was the first movie to utilize this animation to move the creatures. Doyle cameoed in the film as himself.

73. Sherlock Holmes is based on a French man called Eugene Vidocq. He was a criminal who spent time on a maximum-security prison ship. He escaped from prison so many times, he gained a reputation as a genius and the police regularly asked him for help in solving crimes. Eventually, the police freed Vidcocq and hired him as the first private detective. Vidcocq popularised the concept of a crime lab, ballistics, blood spattering, relying on fingerprints, and having a criminal database. Using his methods, the French police arrested about 800 criminals per year.

74. He was approached by London police to help them solve the Jack the Ripper case.

75. He ran for parliament twice.

76. Doyle was friends with Dracula author, Bram Stoker, and was in the same class as Treasure Island writer, Robert Louis Stevenson.

77. Sherlock Holmes takes cocaine in the stories, The Sign of Four and A Scandal in Bohemia. These stories were written before it was common knowledge that cocaine was an addictive drug. In Doyle's time, cocaine was seen as a good remedy for colds and toothaches.

    William Gillette, who played Sherlock in the early 20th century, took cocaine on stage to make the scene more authentic.

78. Since Sherlock Holmes believes "the most rational theory is often the correct one," it's easy to assume Doyle didn't believe in the supernatural. On the contrary, Doyle had such a passionate belief in the paranormal that he was regularly made fun of by his peers. He attended séances to contact his dead son and brother. Although he was good friends with Harry Houdini, they had a falling out because Doyle was certain Houdini had magical powers but pretended his feats were tricks. He also passionately believed in fairies and often defended their existence.

79. He was a skilled skier and wrote about his experience stating it was "getting as near to flying as any earthbound man can. In that glorious air it is a delightful experience." He talked about the sport so much that he is directly responsible for popularising skiing in Switzerland.

80. Doyle resented the Sherlock Holmes stories as he wanted to be known as a historical novelist. He referred to the Holmes books as "hack work" and said he only wrote the stories to pay off college loans.

Arthur Miller

1915 – 2005

Written Work
Death of a Salesman (1949)
The Crucible (1953)
All My Sons (1947)
A View from the Bridge (1955)

81. Arthur Asher Miller's play, Death of a Salesman, premiered on Broadway on February 10th 1949 in Morosco Theatre. The play is often considered to be Miller's greatest work and it won the Pulitzer Prize for Drama.

82. He married Mary Slattery in 1940. In 1951, Miller met Marilyn Monroe and had an affair with her shortly afterwards. Miller left his wife for Monroe and married her in 1956.
    They divorced after five years and Monroe died from a drug overdose 19 months later.
    Miller married a photographer called Inge Morath in 1962. She died in 2002.

83. Miller was of Polish and Jewish descent. Marilyn Monroe wanted to impress Miller's family so she converted to Judaism. After her conversion, Monroe's films were banned in Egypt for many years.

84. He was inspired to become a writer after reading Fyodor Dostoyevsky's The Brothers Karazamov.

85. His daughter, Rebecca, married three-time Oscar winner, Daniel Day-Lewis. Day-Lewis played the lead character in the film adaptation of Miller's play, The Crucible.

86. His Broadway debut was The Man Who Had All the Luck. It failed so badly, it was closed after four performances.

87. He wrote the first draft of Death of a Salesman in less than one day.

88. He travelled to Salem, Massachusetts, to research the witch trials of 1692 for his play, The Crucible. During these trials, innocent people were accused of witchcraft which destroyed trust in the community and led to the hanging of dozens of innocent women. Miller found it interesting that the judges committed evil by attempting to destroy a non-existent evil. He thought it was very similar to the House of Un-American Activities Committee (HUAC) who accused innocent Americans of being spies for Communists without proof. Between 1947-1956, US Senator, Joseph McCarthy, regularly accused Americans of spying for the Soviets with no evidence. This caused countless Americans to turn on one another and was known as The Second Red Scare. To accuse someone of treason without proof is known as McCarthyism.

    When The Crucible debuted in 1953, it was very successful and was met with positive reviews. In 1956, the HUAC subpoenaed Miller to appear before the committee. Miller refused to out any of his colleagues of communicating with Communists and so, he was fined, blacklisted, and was barred a US passport. Although he was given a prison sentence in 1958, his conviction was overturned by the court of appeals.

89. Elia Kazan directed the play, Death of A Salesman. Although Miller was good friends with Elia Kazan, they had a falling out in 1952 when Kazan named eight people to the HUAC who had been in contact with the

Communist Party. Miller didn't speak to Kazan for a decade after this.

90. He died of a heart attack on February 10th 2005. He died on the 56th anniversary of the debut of Death of a Salesman.

Ayn Rand

1905 – 1982

Written Work
Atlas Shrugged (1957)
The Fountainhead (1943)

91. Her real name is Alisa Zinov'yevna Rosenbaum.

92. She was a Russian-American novelist, playwright, screenwriter, and philosopher.

93. Rand was obsessed with stamp-collecting and Scrabble.

94. Rand taught herself to read when she was six.

95. Rand was an extra in the 1927 film, The King of Kings. It was directed by Cecil B. DeMille who is best known for directing The Ten Commandments. While working on the film, Rand met a man called Frank O' Connor. The pair got married in 1929.

96. Rand developed her own philosophical concept called Objectivism. Objectivism is the idea that reality exists outside human consciousness. Although many people find this concept fascinating, it is often dismissed by academic philosophers.

97. Rand moved to the US in 1929 and became a citizen in 1931.

98. Her fourth and final book, Atlas Shrugged, is seen as her magnum opus. The story takes place in a dystopian United States where the country's most powerful industrialists abandon their wealth in

response to stricter regulations on their companies. This, in turn, causes the collapse in many important industries.

The title is a reference to the Ancient Greek Titan, Atlas, who holds the Earth above his shoulders. If Atlas were to "shrug," the world would collapse. However, this metaphor falls apart when you realise that Atlas didn't hold up the Earth according to Ancient Greek myth. Instead, he held up the sky. You'd think the writer would have researched that before she appropriated it for the book's title.

99. She dismissed all forms of religion, which was rare for the time.

100. She smoked so often, she developed lung cancer and had one of her lungs removed. After the operation, Rand still believed there was no "conclusive non-statistical" proof that smoking was harmful to one's health.

Beatrix Potter

1866 – 1943

Written Work
The Tale of Peter Rabbit (1902)

101. Helen Beatrix Potter is best known for writing The Tale of Peter Rabbit. However, Potter was also an illustrator and a mycologist (mushroom biologist.) She was held in high regard due to her knowledge of fungi.

102. She had a pet hedgehog, several mice, and a rabbit called Benjamin Bouncer.

103. In 1905, her editor, Norman Warne, proposed to her but died a month later. She married a solicitor called William Heelis in 1913.

104. She wrote 28 books which sold over 100 million copies. They have been translated into over 35 languages.

105. A film about her life called Miss Potter was made in 2006. Renee Zellweger played the titular character.

106. Walt Disney wanted to make a Peter Rabbit film but Potter didn't give him the rights.

107. Between 1905-1909, Potter bought two farms.

108. She was excellent at managing merchandise and created dolls, Peter Rabbit wall-paper, figurines, tea-sets and board games. She was an excellent artist and so, designed most of the merchandise herself.

109. The Tale of Peter Rabbit was banned in London in 1985 for portraying "middle-class rabbits."

110. She died of pneumonia and heart disease. Her ashes were scattered on her property. Two years later, her land was donated to the National Trust. Most of this land now makes up the Lake District National Park.

Ben Jonson

1572 – 1637

Written Work
Volpone (1605-1606)
Every Man in His Humour (1598)
The Alchemist (1610)

111. Jonson's play, The Isle of Dogs, was so controversial, he was arrested. The play was destroyed and nobody knows what it was about.

112. Although Shakespeare has a reputation for "creating more English words than anyone else," this isn't true. Shakespeare concocted over 2,000 phrases but he only invented 229 words. Jonson, on the other hand, created 558 words. Like Shakespeare, Jonson Anglo-Saxonised many words from Ancient Greek. For example, he took the Greek word "palindromos" and turned it into the English word "palindrome." A palindrome is a word or phrase that reads the same thing if read backwards e.g. dad, civic, A nut for a jar of tuna. Palindromos meant "running back again."

113. Jonson cast William Shakespeare in his play, Every Man in His Humour.

114. He was considered the greatest dramatic genius of the English Renaissance apart from William Shakespeare.

115. His father died when he was only a month old.

116. He married Anna Lewis in 1594. He said his wife was "a shrew, but honest." What a guy.

117. He killed an actor in a duel in 1598.

118. He was writing a drama called Sad Shepherd when he died. It was never completed.

119. Jonson started as an actor in 1597. When he didn't succeed, Jonson decided to take up writing.

120. He suffered several strokes in the 1620s and died in 1637.

Brothers Grimm

Jacob Grimm - 1785 – 1863
Wilhelm Grimm - 1786 – 1859

Written Work
Grimm's Fairy Tales (1812)

121. The Brothers Grimm are famous for their collection of stories that include Snow White, Cinderella, Sleeping Beauty, and many more. However, Jacob and Wilhem Grimm didn't write any of these stories. They collected many folktales and released them as a compendium. This would make the Brothers Grimm lexicographers, not writers.

122. They had seven other siblings.

123. In 1838, the Brothers Grimm started writing the German dictionary. They died before they finished and only got as far as the letter, F. It took 120 years to finish the book.

124. Their birth home was destroyed during World War II.

125. Jacob never married.

126. In 1830, King Augustus demanded that all professors in Gottigen swear allegiance to him. When Jacob and Wilhelm refused, they were fired and nearly deported.

127. The first draft of Grimm's Fairy Tales was called Children's and Household Tales and was made up of 86 stories. By the time the pair died, the collection of their

stories had already gone through seven editions and was made up of 211 stories.

128. The collection was made up of Rapunzel, Hansel and Gretel, Rumpelstiltskin, Sleeping Beauty, and Snow White. The first story in their collection is The Frog King, which was adapted into the Disney film, The Princess and the Frog. The final story in their latest edition is The Hazel Branch.

129. 30 stories were removed from the latest edition including the classic tale, Puss in Boots.

130. Although Disney films like Sleeping Beauty, Cinderella, and Snow White and the Seven Dwarfs are clearly geared to children, the Brothers Grimm stories are vulgar, gory, and disturbing. However, the stories were even more violent and scary before the Brothers Grimm got hold of them. Jacob and Wilhelm were devout Christians and so, altered or removed any story elements that they considered too crass or lewd.

Bram Stoker

1847 – 1912

Written Work
Dracula (1897)

131.   Abraham Stoker was born in Dublin in Ireland.

132.   Throughout his life, Stoker was best known as the personal assistant of the actor, Henry Irving. Stoker was the business manager of Irving's playhouse, the Lyceum Theatre.

   Henry Irving was the main inspiration for the titular character in Dracula (despite the fact that many sources state it was Vlad the Impaler.) Stoker incorporated many of Irving's mannerisms into the iconic character.

133.   Stoker wrote Dracula when he was 50. Although he wrote 11 other novels, nothing had the same effect on literature as Dracula did.

134.   Stoker was inspired to write Dracula after researching Irish folktales about fairies. In Irish folklore, fairies drink blood.

135.   Originally, the Dracula novel was called The Dead Un-Dead.

136.   Originally, the Dracula character was called Wampyr. He changed the name to Dracula, when he learned the Irish for "bad blood" was "Droch Ola."

137.   Dracula has been portrayed in over 220 films, which is more than any other character. Christopher

Lee has portrayed the character 11 times, which is more than any other film actor.

138. Stoker couldn't walk until he was seven years old.

139. Dracula was released as a stage play eight days before it was officially published.

140. It is uncertain what Stoker died from but it was probably syphilis.

CS Lewis

1898 – 1963

Written Work
The Chronicles of Narnia (1950-1956)

141. Clive Stapes Lewis was Irish.

142. When Lewis was four, his dog, Jacksie, was hit by a car. Lewis was so devastated, that he only responded to the name, Jack, for a while. His close friends called him Jack for the rest of his life.

143. He is most famous for writing The Chronicles of Narnia, which is made up of seven books –
i) The Lion, the Witch and the Wardrobe
ii) Prince Caspian
iii) The Voyage of the Dawn Treader
iv) The Silver Chair
v) The Horse and His Boy
vi) The Magician's Nephew
vii) The Last Battle

144. Lewis had to write everything with a pen since he never got the hang of a typewriter.

145. The character, Treebeard, from The Lord of the Rings is based on Lewis.

146. Although critics weren't big fans of The Lion, the Witch and the Wardrobe, readers adored the book and it went on to sell over 85 million copies, making it the ninth most successful novel ever written.

147. Lewis was never rich, simply because he gave so much of his income to charity.

148. After graduating from Oxford, Lewis was offered a teaching position at Magdalen College, Oxford, in 1925. While he was there, Lewis and several other writers formed a book group. This group included JRR Tolkien and Lewis' brother, Warren. The group called themselves The Inklings.

149. During World War II, Lewis broadcast radio shows, most of which revolved around Christian themes.

150. He died on the same day as Aldous Huxley and John F. Kennedy.

Charles Dickens

1812 - 1870

Written Work
A Christmas Carol (1843)
Great Expectations (1960-1861)
Oliver Twist (1837-1839)
David Copperfield (1849-1850)
A Tale of Two Cities (1859)
Little Dorrit (1855-1857)
Bleak House (1852-1853)
Nicholas Nickleby (1838-1839)

151. Charles John Huffam Dickens adored cats and even said, "What greater love than the love of a cat?" Although he owned many felines, his favourite was a deaf cat called Bob. When Bob died, Dickens cut off his paw, and turned it into a letter opener.

152. When Dickens was 12, his father was imprisoned for debt. Dickens dropped out of school and worked at a factory labelling cans to raise enough money to pay his father's bail. Dickens returned to school when he was 15 but dropped out soon after when his family suffered money problems again. Dickens raised money for his father by working in an office. Within a year, Dickens became a freelance reporter.

153. He had ten children with his wife, Catherine. After his wife had her second child, she suffered postpartum depression. This wasn't a recognised disorder at the time and so she received no sympathy from Dickens. He even divided the bedroom in two so he didn't have to see her and kept his children away from her, worried for their well-being.

154. He was accused of having an affair with his sister-in-law. Although this isn't true, Dickens did have an affair with an 18-year-old actress called Ellen Ternan. At the time, Dickens was 45. Dickens wrote stories to her about a knight saving her from dragons and ogres.

This was during the Victorian era, where an affair could destroy a person's reputation beyond repair, so the affair was not in the public eye. It went on for 13 years, until Dicken's death.

155. He had a pet raven called Grip. When Grip died, Dickens commemorated his memory by writing about a talking raven in the book, Barnaby Rudge. One critic liked the book but thought the raven was too sentimental and should've been a more profound character. That critic was Edgar Allen Poe.

156. Due to suffering Obsessive Compulsive Disorder, Dickens had many unusual habits. He rearranged the furniture of every room he resided in, combed his hair hundreds of times daily and insisted that he had to write while facing north.

157. He visited morgues and stared at corpses for hours. When his friend asked why he stared at the dead, Dickens said, "I am dragged by an invisible force into the Morgue."

You know what the weirdest thing is? He visited the morgue on Christmas day. It makes you see A Christmas Carol a little differently, doesn't it?

158. He visited Rome to witness a execution by guillotine. Afterward, Dickens hung around to study the "apparent annihilation of the neck."

159. Dickens died from a stroke while he was halfway through writing his 12-part story, Edwin Drood.

160. He was obsessed with spontaneous combustion and argued with anyone who questioned its existence. He even wrote a passage in one of his novels mocking anyone who doubted this phenomenon.

Charlotte Bronte

1816 – 1855

Written Work
Jane Eyre (1847)

161. Charlotte Bronte had six siblings; Maria, Elizabeth, Patrick, Emily (who wrote Wuthering Heights,) Anne (who wrote Agnes Grey,) and Patrick Branwell. Although Branwell was a writer like Charlotte, Anne, and Emily, his books didn't do well because they were a bit rubbish.

162. Charlotte Bronte popularised the name Shirley due to her novel of the same name.

163. There is a school in Jane Eyre called Lowood. It is based on the Clergy Daughters' School that Charlotte attended as a child. The sadistic director of Lowood, Mr. Brocklehurst, was based on the founder of the Clergy Daughters' School, Reverend W. Carus Wilson.

164. She was only five years old when her mother, Maria, died from ovarian cancer.

165. When Charlotte Bronte was 20 years old, she sent her poems to an English poet called Robert Southey. He wrote back to Charlotte, telling her that she was obviously talented but she should give up since "literature cannot be the business of a woman's life, and it ought not to be."
    To counter this, she used the male pseudonym, Currer Bell, for her writing.

166. When Jane Eyre was published, it was an instant success. One critic said it was "the best novel of the

season." However, some readers considered it to be "anti-Christian."

167. While living in Belgium, she fell in love with a married teacher called Professor Constantin Heger. Although Bronte wrote him letters, Heger tore them up. Her experience of unrequited love was incorporated into her novel, Villette.

168. Charlotte Bronte was 38 when she died. Although that sounds very young, she lived longer than her siblings who all died when they were about 30 years old. Charlotte Bronte was pregnant when she died.

169. All the Brontes died of tuberculosis.

170. She was friends with another writer called Elizabeth Gaskell. When Charlotte died, Gaskell wrote Charlotte's biography, The Life of Charlotte Bronte. It was this book that made Charlotte Bronte a household name rather than the books she wrote while she was alive. Although it's common practice now, the book did well because it emphasised Charlottes private life rather than her writing so the readers saw her as a person rather than as a novelist.

Christopher Marlowe

1564 – 1593

Written Work
The Tragical History of the Life and Death of Doctor Faustus (1588)
Dido, Queen of Carthage (1587-1594)
Tamburlaine the Great (1587-1588)

171. Christopher Marlowe's first play was Dido, Queen of Carthage. Although it was published in 1593, Marlowe performed it with his friends in 1587. Some historians believe Marlowe wrote Dido when he was still a student.

172. He translated poetry from the Roman poet, Ovid.

173. Tamburlaine the Great was a two-part play. It was the last play that Marlowe published while he was still alive.

174. His friends called him Kit, Marcarde, Mercury, and The Muses' Darling.

175. In 1593, Marlowe was arrested for the crime of atheism. The penalty for this crime was being burnt at the stake. However, Marlowe was released on the condition that he reported to a court officer daily.

176. It is uncertain exactly when Marlowe was born but he was baptised on February 26th 1564. It was customary at the time to be baptised three days after birth so Marlowe was probably born in February 23st 1564. He was born the same year as William Shakespeare.

177. On May 30th 1593, Marlowe had dinner with a government employee called Ingram Frizer. After arguing over who should pay the bill, Ingram stabbed Marlowe above his right eye. Although this is considered to be the official way that Marlowe died, there is a conflicting story that he was killed in a dining-house by a group of men. Marlowe was only 29 when he died.

178. Marlowe was buried in an unmarked grave in St. Nicholas' Church in Deptford on June 1st 1593.

179. There have been rumours for centuries that Marlowe was a secret agent. When he was in Cambridge, it was unknown how he was paying for his studies. Also, he was absent for months at a time with no explanation. Some historians have theorised that he was absent due to being on "missions" and his secret agency gave Marlowe an income. Some have speculated that the Queen ordered Marlowe's death.

180. Another conspiracy theory suggests that Marlowe faked his death and took on the name of another Elizabethan playwright – William Shakespeare! This conspiracy is known as the Marlovian theory. The first time that William Shakespeare's name was ever referenced was in his work, Venus and Adonis. This was published about a week or two after the apparent death of Marlowe.

Although the authors' works have similarities, this theory has never been taken seriously after 16 jurors accepted Marlowe's death at an inquest held by the Queen's personal coroner.

Chuck Palahniuk

1962 –

Written Work
Fight Club (1996)
Choke (2001)

181. Chuck Palahniuk was camping when he got into a fight. When Palaniuk went back to work, he was visibly bruised but nobody said anything to him. Instead, his co-workers made superficial small talk with him. This inspired Palahniuk to write the book, Fight Club.

182. His parents were Carol Adele and Fred Palahniuk. Fred witnessed his own father kill Fred's mother before committing suicide. Years later, Fred and his girlfriend were murdered by her ex-boyfriend.

183. Fight Club started off as a short story. This short story became Chapter 6.

184. His first novel was Fight Club. It was adapted into a film in 1999. Sadly, nobody knew how to market the film and it tanked at the box office. It is now considered to be one of the best films ever and Palahniuk has admitted that he prefers it to the novel.

185. In Fight Club, Tyler Durden forms a cult-like organization called Project Mayhem that intends to bring down modern civilization. This was based on Palahniuk's own experience when he was a member of a prankster group called the Cacophony Symphony.

186. He didn't start writing until he was in his 30s.

187. He is related to the Oscar-winning actor, Jack Palance.

188. He is so meticulous with his writing that he calls his method "Drowning in Detail."

189. He worked at a homeless shelter and a hospice. He had to drive terminally ill people to meetings. He incorporated these experiences into Fight Club.

190. He is incredibly protective of his private life. Although rumours circulated that he is gay for years, Palahniuk only openly admitted it in 2008.

Cormac McCarthy

1933 –

Written Work
The Road (2006)
All the Pretty Horses (1992)
No Country for Old Men (2005)

191.   His real name is Charles McCarthy. "Cormac" means "son of Charles."

192.   His novel, The Road, won a Pulitzer in 2007. It revolves around a father desperately trying to protect his son in a post-apocalyptic world. It was adapted into a film in 2009.

193.   His novel, No Country for Old Men, started off as a screenplay in the 1980s. It was adapted into a film in 2007 and was directed by the Coen Brothers.

194.   McCarthy's first novel was The Orchard Keeper. He sent it to the publishing agency, Random House, because "it was the only publisher I had heard of."

195.   McCarthy used to be a heavy drinker but has been a teetotaller since he was in his 40s.

196.   He wrote the script for the film, The Counsellor, which starred Brad Pitt, Cameron Diaz, Javier Bardem, and Michael Fassbender. Despite a stellar cast, it received scathing reviews.

197.   Although he has been writing for 40 years, McCarthy didn't give an interview until 2007. When McCarthy was asked why he avoids the spotlight, the reclusive author said, "I don't think it's good for your

head. If you spend a lot of time writing about a book, you probably shouldn't be talking about it, you should be doing it."

198. He didn't have an agent for most of his career.

199. He wrote a play called The Sunset Limited in 2006. It was adapted into a film in 2011. The only actors in the film are Samuel L. Jackson and Tommy Lee Jones.

200. He used the same typewriter for almost 50 years.

Daniel Defoe

1660 – 1731

Written Work
The Life and Strange Adventures of Robinson Crusoe (1719)

201. His birth name is Daniel Foe. He changed his surname to "DeFoe" to make it sound more aristocratic.

202. He was a close friend to King William III and became his personal spy.

203. Defoe's most renowned work is Robinson Crusoe. Although Robinson Crusoe influenced many great stories like Gulliver's Travels and Lord of the Flies, it has a lot of plot holes and glaring errors.
    On page 53-54, the titular character fills his pockets with food...while he is naked. Here's the passage – "I pulled off my clothes...and took the water." When he arrives at the sunken ship, it reads, "I went to the bread room and filled my pockets with biscuit... I had the mortification to see my coat, shirt, and waistcoat... swim away: as for my breeches... I swam on board in them, and my stockings."
    At one point, Crusoe says he wishes he had ink. Later in the story, Crusoe obtains ink but never explains how. Although Crusoe saved a pipe from the shipwreck, he complains that he doesn't have a pipe later in the story.

204. Robinson Crusoe coined the term "Robinsade" which refers to how a person acts differently in solitude compared to how one acts in society. This applies to other stories like Lord of the Flies or the TV show, Lost.

205. Robinson Crusoe is written as if it is a biographical account of Crusoe rather than Defoe telling a story.

Readers loved this as it gave the impression the novel was based on true events.

206. Some people consider Robinson Crusoe as the first English novel.

207. Even the biggest fans of Defoe's work don't know that Robinson Crusoe is a trilogy. The second book is called The Farther Adventures of Robinson Crusoe: Being the Second and Last Part of His Life, And of the Strange Surprising Accounts of his Travels Round three Parts of the Globe. It came out the same year as its predecessor. The trilogy concluded in Serious Reflections of Robinson Crusoe in 1720.

208. Defoe was 59 when he wrote Robinson Crusoe.

209. Defoe was never financially secure and spent time in prison due to his debts.

210. Although it's common practice for a writer to use a fake name, Defoe might have the world record since he wrote under 198 pseudonyms.

Dante Alighieri

1265 – 1321

Written Work
The Divine Comedy (1308-1320)

211. Durante "Dante" degli Alighieri is best known for writing Comedia (which was later retitled as The Divine Comedy." It is made up of three parts – Inferno, Purgatorio, and Paradiso. The first part is the most famous and is better known as Dante's Inferno.

212. The Divine Comedy is 14,233 lines long.

213. Few people could read The Divine Comedy at first since it was originally written in Latin. As a result, Dante decided to create a new language that was easy to learn. You may have heard of this language. It's called Italian. Dante is known as The Father of the Italian Language. In French, "Italian" is translated into "la langue de Dante." Because of this, common people could read his books.

214. In his youth, Dante fell for a girl called Beatrice. When she died, Dante was so devastated that it inspired him to resurrect her as a character in his work. In The Divine Comedy, he finds her soul in Hell and sends it through Purgatory and into Heaven. His love for Beatrice allowed him to create the greatest poem of the medieval era and the greatest literature in Italian history.

215. Inferno, Purgatorio, and Paradiso all end with the same word – stars.

216. Renowned poet, TS Eliot, only learned to speak Italian to read Dante's work.

217. In the 21st century, there were 50 different English translations of The Divine Comedy.

218. The painter, Michelangelo, listened to a reading of Dante's Inferno as he painted The Last Judgement in the Sistine Chapel.

219. Although Dante will always be known for The Divine Comedy, he also wrote The New Life, On Eloquence in the Vernacular.

220. Dante supposedly died of malaria when he was 56 years old.

Douglas Adams

1952 – 2001

Written Work
The Hitchhiker's Guide to the Galaxy (1978-1980)
Dirk Gently's Holistic Detective Agency (1987)
The Meaning of Liff (1983)

221. He is most famous for his novel, The Hitchhiker's Guide to the Galaxy series –
    i) The Hitchhiker's Guide to the Galaxy
    ii) The Restaurant at the End of the Universe
    iii) Life, the Universe and Everything
    iv) So Long, and Thanks for All the Fish
    v) Most Harmless
    However, it was a radio show before it was a novel. He went on to write four sequels. He called them A Trilogy in Five Parts.
        The series had another sequel called And Another Thing but it was written eight years after Adams died.

222. He wrote sketches for Monty Python's Flying Circus.

223. He wrote three Doctor Who specials – The Pirate Planet, City of Death, and Shada.

224. The Hitchhiker's Guide to the Galaxy was a #1 best-seller in the UK and sold 15 million copies in the UK alone. Three of his books became New York Times bestsellers.

225. Adams looked like a professional bodybuilder. He stood 6ft 5 and regularly worked out.

226. Since his full name was Douglas Noel Adams, his friends called him DNA.

227. The main character in The Hitchhiker's Guide to the Galaxy is Arthur Dent. One day before Adams died, an asteroid was named Arthurdent in Adams' honour.

228. When asked how he came up with ideas, Adams said he would shower with very hot water and he wouldn't turn it off until he came up with a good idea. His water bill was extremely high.

229. After Douglas Adams became successful, he didn't have much impulse to write any more. His publisher, Sue Freestone, wasn't going to let Adams retire anytime soon and demanded that he kept on writing. When Adams refused, she squatted at his house and bullied him into writing.

   The weirdest thing is this isn't the only time a publisher did this. Another publisher, Sonny Mehta, locked Adams in his hotel room for two weeks without having access to a phone. If he was let out, Adams had to be supervised before being put back in his room to continue writing. When he was asked about the experience, Adams said, "It was simple. I sat at the desk and typed and Sonny sat in an armchair and glowered."

   So if you enjoyed Adams' books, you should thank his kidnapper.

230. Douglas Adams died from a heart attack at the age of 49 while he was working out in the gym. His book, The Salmon of Doubt, was published the year after his death. It was composed of a collection of sketches and an unfinished novel.

Dr. Seuss

1904 – 1991

Written Work
The Cat in the Hat (1957)
How the Grinch Stole Christmas! (1957)
Green Eggs and Ham (1960)
Horton Hears a Who! (1955)

231. His real name is Theodore Geisel.

232. Geisel sold war bonds when he was a boy scout. Geisel was so good at it, he and nine other boy scouts were rewarded with a medal from President Teddy Roosevelt. However, Roosevelt only had nine medals. When he got to Geisel, Roosevelt had nothing to offer him. Geisel was so humiliated, he developed a phobia about crowds for the rest of his life. Geisel rarely gave speeches and spent many years living alone on a mountain top.

233. He was the editor-in-chief of the comedy magazine, The Jack-o-Lantern. Geisel was fired for drinking during the Prohibition Era when the purchase of alcohol was illegal. Worried that his name was tarnished, he decided to continue writing under the pseudonym, Dr. Seuss.

234. His editor bet Seuss that he couldn't write a book using 50 different words or less. Seuss accomplished this with his classic story, Green Eggs and Ham.

235. The director of education division at Houghton Mifflin challenged Seuss to write a book using 236 words that the director believed were the most important words to a first-grader. Nine months later, Seuss finished the book – The Cat in the Hat.

236. The 1950 short film, Gerald McBoing-Boing, won an Oscar for Best Animated Short Film. It is based on one of Seuss' stories.

237. Seuss invented the word "nerd." It first appeared in the 1950 book, If I Ran the Zoo.

238. He created several World War II propaganda cartoons for the New York Daily newspaper. These cartoons depicted the Japanese as racially insensitive, which Seuss regretted after the destruction of Hiroshima and Nagasaki. This inspired him to write Horton Hears a Who! in 1954. The story revolves around an elephant called Horton trying to protect a tiny planet full of beings called Whos. Because of the elephant's giant ears, only Horton can hear the Whos pleas not to hurt them. Since nobody else can hear the Whos, everyone thinks Horton is making it up. Since Horton knows the Whos are real, he does everything in his power to prove their existence. This story is a metaphor for the Japanese people who tried to make the world aware of the long-term effects of the attacks on Japan.

Seuss dedicated the book to "My Great Friend, Mitsugi Nakamura of Kyoto, Japan." Kyoto was the city that was originally supposed to be bombed instead of Hiroshima. The Americans changed their minds at the last minute because Kyoto was too cloudy to fly over.

239. His wife, Helen, died from cancer in 1967. He married Audrey Stone Diamond the following year.

240. He died of oral cancer at the age of 87.

Edgar Allen Poe

1809-1849

Written Work
The Raven (1845)
The Tell-Tale Heart (1843)
The Pit and the Pendulum (1842)

241. Edgar Poe's parents were actors. They were performing in King Lear the same year Edgar was born. Since Edgar is a character in King Lear, it's possible Poe was named after him.

242. He lost his parents and brother at a young age.

243. After his family died, Poe was taken in by John and Frances Allan (although they never officially adopted him.) They had a falling out since Poe gambled all their money away. He was kicked out and never spoke to them again. However, he took on their surname as part of his pseudonym as an author.

244. Edgar Allen Poe made $9 for his poem, The Raven.

245. He only wrote one play in 1835 called Politian.

246. The most iconic photo of Poe shows him looking dishevelled, baggy-eyed and miserable. This picture probably became popular because it perfectly encapsulates the crippling anxiety and dread that is associated with his work. However, Poe was handsome and athletic. He had a reputation for being sporty and held a record for swimming six miles up the James River in Virginia.

247. Poe was 26 when he married his cousin, Virginia. She

was only 13. After four years of marriage, she died of tuberculosis.

248. His only novel was The Narrative of Arthur Gordon Pym. Although Poe claimed it was based on a true story, it wasn't…at first.

It was about four survivors of a shipwreck who were in an open boat for many days before they decided to kill and eat the cabin boy whose name was Richard Parker. In 1884, the Mignonette yacht crashed, leaving all but four people dead. Starving, three of the survivors ate the other who happened to be the cabin boy. The boy's name was Richard Parker.

249. Poe was fascinated by space and cosmology. In his final piece, Eureka, he hypothesized the universe started from a single point 80 years before the Big Bang Theory was strongly considered by the scientific community.

250. On October 3rd 1849, Poe was found on the streets in desperate need of medical attention. He died four days later in hospital. When he was found, Poe was wearing clothes that weren't his own and he kept crying out for a man called Reynolds. No one knows who Reynolds was.

For almost 150 years, no one had a clue what Poe died from. However, this mystery was solved in 1996. Several doctors were given anonymous patients with a list of symptoms. Unbeknownst to Dr. R. Michael Benitez, he was given Poe along with the symptoms he suffered before his death. According to Benitez, Poe was "a clear case of rabies."

Edgar Rice Burroughs

1875 – 1950

Written Work
Tarzan series (1912-1995)
Barsoom series (1917-1964)

251. Edgar Rice Burroughs is best known for writing 24 novels about Tarzan.

252. In the novels, "Tarzan" means "white-skinned." Tarzan was named by his adoptive mother, Kala the ape. Burroughs based the name on a southern Californian region called Tarzana. Burroughs adored Tarzana and purchased land there later in his life.

253. Many people believe Tarzan was raised by gorillas. In the novels, he was brought up by a fictional ape called a mangani. They're bigger than gorillas and can speak.

254. Tarzan's real name is John Clayton Greystoke. Since his parents were aristocrats, Tarzan is sometimes called Lord Greystoke. However, Tarzan states that he is a viscount, not a lord. A viscount is a title in Europe of a lower-middling rank.

255. Burroughs wrote the Barsoom series. The story revolves around a soldier that is transported to Mars and becomes a hero to its people. It was adapted into the film, John Carter, in 2012. It lost approximately $209 million, making it one of the most unsuccessful films ever.

    Weirdly, Walt Disney strongly considered adapting this story before deciding to make Snow White and the Seven Dwarfs. If he adapted A Princess of Mars, and it failed at the box office, Walt Disney would've gone bankrupt and Disney Studios probably wouldn't exist.

256. He wrote A Princess of Mars under the pseudonym, Normal Bean. His publishers assumed this was a typo and changed it to Norman Bean.

257. Burroughs sold pencil sharpeners before he was a successful writer.

258. His great-grandson is the film director, Wes Anderson.

259. Joseph Stalin's favourite author was Edgar Rice Burroughs.

260. He died at the age of 74 from a heart attack. At the time of his death, Burroughs was the world's best-selling author.

Emily Bronte

1818 – 1848

Written Work
Wuthering Heights (1847)

261. Emily Bronte was the fifth of six children.

262. Emily and her sisters wrote a collection of poems but only managed to sell two copies.

263. She wrote under the pseudonym, Ellis Bell.

264. Wuthering Heights was rejected many times because Emily Bronte was a woman. A publisher accepted it after Emily bribed him with £50, which was a large sum at the time.

265. Her father had no idea that Emily was writing Wuthering Heights. He never read it after it was published.

266. Emily's brother, Branwell, suffered from alcoholism. This was incorporated into the character of Hindley Earnshaw in Wuthering Heights.

267. In Wuthering Heights, Dr. Kenneth only appears to confirm that a character has died or is dying. Because many people died in Emily's life, she always associated doctors with death. When she fell ill with tuberculosis, she refused to see a doctor, believing he symbolised her inevitable demise.

268. In 1848, Emily's brother passed away. While at Branwell's funeral, Emily got a cold. It developed into tuberculosis and she died the same year. Of the 12

characters that die in Wuthering Heights, three of them perished from tuberculosis.

269. She published Wuthering Heights only one year before she passed away.

270. Unlike her sister's novel, Jane Eyre, Wuthering Heights was not an immediate success and Emily never experienced the influence of her story.

Emily Dickinson

1830 – 1886

Written Work
A lot

271. Emily Elizabeth Dickinson wrote over 1,800 poems. Only 11 of them were published during her lifetime –
    i)   Magnum bonum
    ii)   Sic transit Gloria mundi
    iii)   Nobody knows this little Rose
    iv)   I taste a liquor never brewed
    v)   Sage in their Alabaster Chamber
    vi)   Flowers – Well – if anybody
    vii)   These are the days when Birds come back
    viii)   Some keep the Sabbath going to church
    ix)   Blazing in Gold - and
    x)   Success is counted sweetest
    xi)   A narrow Fellow in / the grass.

272. She rarely titled her work. Most of the "titles" are simply the first line of each poem.

273. Most of Dickinson's poems were written in the second-floor bedroom of her home.

274. Her father, Edward, was a politician.

275. Her grandfather, Samuel, founded Amherst College, which Dickinson attended for seven years.

276. Dickinson was very particular how she wanted her funeral. Dickinson requested a white colour theme and she had a preferred path to the cemetery.

277. Many of her poems were altered against her wishes by publishers to match "poetic trends." Also, she didn't use punctuation or capitalization which also had to be changed. Some of her poems were published anonymously, which was sadly common for the time for female writers.

278. Before she died, Dickinson begged her sister, Lavinia, to torch all her work. When Lavinia saw that her sister had written 40 volumes of work, she couldn't bring herself to destroy them.

279. Her poetry was published four years after she died. Although it was criticized at first, she is now considered to be one of the greatest American poets ever.

280. Her entire collection wasn't available until 1955, 69 years after she passed away.

Ernest Hemingway

1899 – 1961

Written Work
The Old Man and the Sea (1952)
The Sun Also Rises (1926)
A Farewell to Arms (1929)

281. Ernest Hemingway hunted sharks with machine guns. Once, he shot himself in both legs while wrestling a shark.

282. The first successful novel that Hemingway wrote was The Sun Also Rises. After he became known as a talented writer, the publisher, Boni & Liveright, asked Hemingway to sign with them. Hemingway didn't realise that his contract with the publisher made Boni & Liveright receive almost all the money from the next three books he wrote. Enraged, Hemingway wrote the worst book possible – The Torrents of Spring. He wrote the whole thing in 11 days. Worried that Boni & Liveright might sue him, Hemingway got renowned writer, F. Scott Fitzgerald, to publicly declare the book a masterpiece. Liveright dropped the deal and Hemingway went with another publisher.

283. He used to be an ambulance driver in Italy during World War I.

284. He was a war correspondent during World War II.

285. While he was on vacation in Pamplona in Spain, Hemingway fell in love with bull-fighting. He befriended several matadors and eventually took part in several bull-fighting competitions. He even wrote about the sport in his 1926 story, The Sun Also Rises.

286. He famously said, "Always do sober what you said you'd do drunk. That'll teach ya to keep your mouth shut."

287. Hemingway became paranoid in his later life and was convinced he was bugged by "the feds." Although this sounds like a typical example of mental instability, he was right. The bureau's director, J. Edgar Hoover, bugged Hemingway's phones, audited his accounts, and had him followed. Hoover wrote a 127-page document detailing any suspicious behavior by Hemingway.

    But why were the FBI so paranoid about a writer? Well...

288. Hemingway was a KGB spy. According to documents retrieved by the former KGB agent, Alexander Vassiliev, Hemingway met with Soviet agents and stated he was more than happy to help them. He was given the codename, Argo, and began working with the Soviets. However, they let him go shortly afterwards since all his intel was unhelpful and useless.

289. Although his paranoia was justified, nobody believed that Hemingway was under surveillance. As a result, his family put him in a psychiatric hospital where we underwent electric shock therapy. The treatment seemed to make him more unstable as Hemingway repeatedly tried to take his life. Sadly, he eventually succeeded.

290. Ernest Hemingway committed suicide, as did his father, sister, brother, son, and granddaughter.

F. Scott Fitzgerald

1896 – 1940

Written Work
The Great Gatsby (1925)
The Last Tycoon (1941)

291. His full name was Francis Scott Key Fitzgerald. He was named after Francis Scott Key, who wrote the lyrics for the Star-Spangled Banner.

292. He took up writing when he attended Princeton. His first novel, The Side of Paradise, was published in 1920 and was an instant success.

293. Fitzgerald lived in Hollywood after he was hired as a scriptwriter by MGM in the 1930s. He was a script doctor and rewrote scenes to avoid clunky dialogue or blatant plot holes. He tweaked the script for the film, Gone with the Wind.

294. From 1920 to 1940, Fitzgerald moved to a new house every few years from 1920 to 1940. In this time, he lived in Paris, Rome, LA, Delaware, Long Island, Minnesota, Connecticut, New York, Baltimore, North Carolina, and Switzerland.

295. He was friends with legendary writer, Ernest Hemingway. Hemingway hated Fitzgerald's wife, Zelda, calling her "crazy" and a distraction from Fitzgerald's work.

296. His pride and joy was his novel, The Great Gatsby. It was nearly called Gold-Hatted Gatsby, The High-Bouncing Lover, Trimalchio, Along the Ash Heaps and Millionaires, and Incident at West Egg.

297. Fitzgerald was an atrocious speller and probably suffered from dyslexia.

298. If you look closely at the front cover of The Great Gatsby, you can see a naked woman in each eye.

299. His wife, Zelda Sayre, died in a fire at the Highland Mental Hospital.

300. F. Scott Fitzgerald only made $13 from The Great Gatsby. Fitzgerald was so devastated by the book's failure, he became an alcoholic. His drinking led to a fatal heart attack when he was only 44.

Frank Herbert

1920 – 1986

Written Work
Dune series (1965-1985)
WorShip series (1965-1988)
ConSentiency series (1970-1977)

301. Frank Herbert's most famous work is the Dune series. The story revolves around a spice called melange, which is the most valuable commodity in the universe. This material only grows on the planet of Arrakis, where most of the story takes place. The spice allows the consumer to live for an extended period of time and see into the future. Herbert said he came up with this idea after consuming many, many, many magic mushrooms.

302. In Dune, an evil galactic federation tries to control the melange but a small group of rebels on a desert planet challenge the evil overlords. After George Lucas read the book, it inspired him to write Star Wars.

303. Herbert wanted to become a writer when he was eight years old.

304. It took six years to write Dune.

305. Dune was rejected nearly 20 times.

306. He served with the US Navy and worked as a photographer for six months during WWII.

307. Dune had a sequel called Children of Dune. It was the first science fiction novel ever to become a New York Times bestseller.

308. Dune was adapted into a film in 1984. It tanked at the box office and was met with mediocre reviews.

309. He was a distant relative of Joseph McCarthy, a Republican Senator who blacklisted countless Americans as suspected Communists.

310. He died at the age of 65 from pancreatic cancer.

Franz Kafka

1883 – 1924

Written Work
The Metamorphosis (1915)
The Trial (1925)

311. Although his family was wealthy, Franz Kafka had a traumatic childhood. His mother worked long hours so he was cared for by servants and maids throughout most of his youth. His father despised Kafka's love of literature which made him feel inadequate about his writing.

312. He was born in in Bohemia in Austria-Hungary (now known as the Czech Republic.)

313. He often wrote about faceless bureaucracies overpowering the common man in an over-the-top surreal manner. Kafka popularised the faceless bureaucracy concept and it has been used in The Prisoner, The Twilight Zone, Dark City, and Brazil.

314. His handwritten manuscript of The Trial was sold in 1988 for $1.98 million.

315. He never married, nor had children.

316. He worked as an insurance officer.

317. His most famous story is Die Verwandlung, (better known as The Metamorphosis.) The story revolves around Gregor Samsa who wakes up to learn he has turned into a gigantic bug. His family are horrified and don't know what to do with him. Sometimes they feed him; other times they barricade or attack him. The book

was a parallel to how people were shunned and ostracised after they were infected with tuberculosis. Speaking of which...

318.   Kafka developed tuberculosis when he was 38. It got so bad, he was unable to work. It took its toll on his mind and left him with insomnia, anxiety, migraines, and depression.

319.   Although many sources state that Kafka died from tuberculosis, he died from starvation. His throat was so swollen, he couldn't eat anything in the last few weeks of his life.

320.   At the time of his death, Kafka hadn't published anything. Just before he died, Kafka asked his friend to burn all his work. His friend refused and had Kafka's work published. Not only is he now considered to be one of the greatest writers ever, his style coined the term, Kafkaesque.

Fyodor Dostoevsky

1821 – 1881

Written Work
Crime and Punishment (1867)
The Idiot (1868-1869)
The Brothers Karamazov (1879-1880)

321. Fyodor Mikhailovich Dostoevsky suffered many tragedies from an early age. His father, Mikhail, died when Dostoevsky was young. It's likely that Mikhail was murdered by a serf. Soon after, Dostoevsky witnessed a serf being assaulted which traumatized him. He developed epileptic seizures the same year.

    At 16, Dostoevsky was devastated when his favourite author, Alexander Pushkin, was killed in a duel. Later that year, Dostoevsky's mother died.

322. Dostoevsky became indirectly involved in a revolutionary movement, where he was arrested, convicted of treason, and sentenced to death. He was blindfolded, ready to be shot by a firing squad when his execution was called off. Instead, he was exiled to Siberia where he was imprisoned for five years. During this time, Dostoevsky's health deteriorated and his epilepsy became exacerbated. He was eventually released by the Tsar.

323. His crippling gambling addiction inspired him to write The Gambler in 1867.

324. His most famous work is Crime and Punishment. Although it is now perceived as a masterpiece, some critics saw it as a political pamphlet. Renowned author, Vladimir Nabokov, considered it too philosophical to be artistic.

325. Crime and Punishment was released in 12 instalments in a journal called The Russian Messenger.

326. Although he considered himself a devout Christian, Dostoevsky rarely attended church and admitted he disliked priests. He usually prayed while looking at the stars.

327. His books have been translated into 170 languages.

328. There are over two dozen film adaptations of Crime and Punishment.

329. Albert Einstein and Friedrich Nietzsche's favourite writer was Fyodor Dostoevsky.

330. He died at the age of 59 after suffering emphysema and a lung haemorrhage.

Geoffrey Chaucer

1343 – 1400

Written Work
The Canterbury Tales (1387-1400)
The Book of the Duchess (1368-1372)
Troilus and Criseyde (1385)

331. Geoffrey Chaucer coined many words including "bagpipe," "universe," and "twitter."

332. His most famous work is The Canterbury Tales. Although it is made up of 24 stories and runs over 17,000 lines long, it was supposed to be composed of 120 stories. The book is presented as part of a storytelling competition where a group of pilgrims travel from London to Canterbury to see the shrine of Saint Thomas Becket at Canterbury Cathedral. Since Chaucer died before completing it, the characters never arrive at Canterbury.

333. In 1366, Chaucer married Sir Payne Roet's daughter, Philippa Roet. Her wealth allowed him to pursue writing. When she died in 1387, he lived off her royalties while he wrote. Shortly afterwards, he gained enough of a reputation to make a steady income.

334. Chaucer is nicknamed the Father of English Literature and is seen as the greatest English poet during the Middle Ages.

335. Although the Book of the Duchess was completed in 1372, it wasn't published for 160 years.

336. He was a clerk for Edward III and Richard II. He gave up the job after being robbed twice.

337. He travelled on diplomatic missions to France, Italy, and Spain.

338. In 1359, Chaucer fought in the Hundred Years' War (which lasted 116 years.) He was captured and held for ransom.

339. It is unclear how Chaucer died but some historians believe he may have been assassinated by political opponents.

340. When Chaucer died, his gravestone became the first of what is known as the Poet's Corner of Westminster Abbey.

George Bernard Shaw

1343 – 1400

Written Work
Pygmalion (1912)
Androcles and the Lion (1913)
Back to Methuselah (1922)
Saint Joan (1923)

341. Geoffrey Bernard Shaw was born in Dublin, Ireland.

342. Pygmalion was adapted into a film in 1938 and remade into the 1964 classic, My Fair Lady.

343. He won a Nobel Prize for Literature in 1925 and won an Oscar for Pygmalion in 1938. He is the first person in history to win both these awards. Bob Dylan became the second person to accomplish this feat in 2016.

344. He was friends with Harpo Marx from the Marx Brothers.

345. George Bernard Shaw famously said, "He who can, does. He who cannot, teaches."

346. He wrote 63 plays.

347. He wrote columns under the name Corno di Bassetto.

348. Shaw was a vegetarian.

349. He died after he fell off a ladder.

350. When he died, his will stipulated that his fortune should be used to create a 40-letter alphabet to replace the current one. Surprisingly, it didn't catch on.

George Orwell

1903 - 1950

Written Work
Animal Farm (1945)
Nineteen Eighty-Four (1949)

351. He was born in India while it was ruled by Britain.

352. His birth name was Eric Arthur Blair. His pen name was inspired by the River Orwell in Suffolk, England.

353. Animal Farm revolves around a group of farm animals that revolt against their human owner but then become corrupted by power. The story is written so simply, a child could easily read it. However, the novel's themes run much deeper. The story is an anti-Soviet satire about Leon Trotsky and Joseph Stalin. The novel did extremely well and made Orwell famous.

354. Although he is best known for writing Animal Farm and Nineteen Eighty-Four, Orwell wrote four other books – Burmese Days, A Clergyman's Daughter, Keep the Aspidistra Flying, and Coming Up for Air.

355. Orwell coined several words including "doublethink," and "newspeak." He said "doublethink means the power of holding two contradictory beliefs in one's mind simultaneously, and accepting both of them." This is also the definition for "cognitive dissonance."

356. Orwell provided the government with a list of people he believed to be Communist including Charlie Chaplin.

357. In the novel, Nineteen Eighty-Four, Room 101 is a room where a person must experience his greatest fear. Orwell came up with the concept when he worked with the BBC and couldn't stand the tedious meetings.

358. He wrote Animal Farm in 1945; the same year that World War II ended. Orwell wrote it "to fuse political purpose and artistic purpose into one whole."

359. Okay, here's a question. What does "Orwellian" mean? If a book is described as Orwellian, does that mean it has the same writing style as Orwell or it covers the same themes like dystopias and dictatorships? Calling someone an Orwellian can be an insult because it can mean that person embraces actions that Orwell condemned. However, calling someone an Orwellian can be a compliment as it can mean that person is being compared to George Orwell. Despite his legacy, nobody can agree on the definition of "Orwellian."

360. Although Orwell developed tuberculosis in 1938, it wasn't diagnosed until 1947. He died in 1950 when an artery burst in his lungs. He was only 46.

George RR Martin

1948 -

Written Work
A Song of Ice and Fire series (1996)

361. George Raymond Richard Martin said that the Breaking Bad character, Walter White, is a more evil character than "anyone in Westeros."

362. He wrote for the 1987 TV series, Beauty and the Beast, with Ron Perlman playing the Beast.

363. He was a writer of the rebooted version of The Twilight Zone that was supposed to run during the 1980s. However, the show was cancelled.

364. He began writing Game of Thrones in 1991. It wasn't published until 1996. He was 48 at the time.

365. He is a huge comic book fan and owns the first issue of The Amazing Spider-Man and Fantastic Four. He used to write to the writers of Fantastic Four when he was a teenager to point out the plot-holes in the stories.
    Also, when Comic-Con opened in 1964, he was the first person to sign up to enter the convention.

366. When Martin was asked how he writes female characters so well, he said, "Well, I've always thought of women as people."

367. He can only type with one finger at a time.

368. Unlike many writers, Martin doesn't write using Microsoft Word. Instead, he uses a program called

WordStar. If you have never heard of it, that's because WordStar hasn't been updated since 1987! The reason why Martin doesn't use updated software is because he doesn't like how modern writing programs automatically capitalize words and underline spelling errors. He may be unaware that these options can be turned off.

369. When English producer, George Martin, died in 2016, Game of Thrones fans panicked, believing that George RR Martin died, meaning his book series would never be completed. Martin had to make an announcement to confirm that he was very much alive.

370. It takes George RR Martin about six years to write a book. Many fans have grown so impatient at the release of his next book in A Song of Ice and Fire series, readers tracked down Martin and begged him to write the next book immediately. Martin then asked them who their favourite character was and then threatened to kill off that character in the next book if the fans didn't leave him alone.

HG Wells

1866 - 1946

Written Work
War of the Worlds (1898)
The Time Machine (1895)
The Invisible Man (1897)
The Island of Doctor Moreau (1896)

371. Herbert George Wells married his cousin Isabel in 1891. He divorced her three years later after falling in love with a student called Amy Robbins. They married in 1895 and had two sons called George Philip and Frank Richard.

372. Wells had a daughter with Amber Reeves in 1909 called Anna-Jane. He also had a son called Anthony with Rebecca West in 1914.

373. Wells drew 650 doodles which he called picshuas. Some of these doodles revolve around his affairs and he depicted his wife as a dictator in these drawings.

374. In 1877, astronomer, Giovanni Schiaparelli, saw channels on Mars. Because he was Italian, he used the words "canali" to describe the channels. 18 years later, an American astronomer called Percival Lowell read Schiaparelli's notes and thought "canali" meant "canals," which can only be made by intelligent life. This inspired HG Wells' novel, War of the Worlds.

375. His novel, The World Set Free, was written in 1914. In the novel, uranium-based grenades called atomic bombs are used in warfare. They are described as a weapon that could cause incalculable damage. This was written 30 years before atomic bombs existed.

376. In 1918, Florence Deeks presented her history manuscript to McMillan and Company. Although it was rejected, the company accepted HG Wells' book, The Outline of History, in 1919. Not only were many passages identical to Deeks' manuscript, it had the exact same mistakes.

377. He was nicknamed Your Lord, the Jaguar. He came up with the nickname.

378. He ran for Parliament in 1922 and 1923 as a Labour Party candidate but didn't get enough votes.

379. He wrote over 114 books in his lifetime.

380. His final words were, "Go away, I'm alright."

HP Lovecraft

1890 - 1937

Written Work
The Call of Cthulhu (1928)
At the Mountains of Madness (1936)

381. Howard Phillips Lovecraft is most famous for writing the Cthulhu mythos. In Lovercraft's stories, Cthulhu (pronounced "Khlul-hloo) was a colossal octopus-faced entity that ruled the world with his race of Ancient Ones long before humanity. Cthulhu is derived from the Greek word "chthonic" which means "subterranean."

    Other stories that revolve around otherworldly cosmic beings are often described as Lovecraftian.

382. Edgar Allen Poe was his favourite writer.

383. One of his most famous books is Necronomicon. It means "an image of the law of the dead." In the context of the story, it was written by "The Mad Arab" in the 8th century and is filled with evil spells. A book by the same name appears in the movie series, The Evil Dead.

384. Although he was a passionate anti-Semite, he married a Jew.

385. Lovecraft was terrified of the cold and collapsed if he felt the slightest chill.

386. He regularly stayed awake for 36 hours straight without the slightest sign of fatigue. Once, he stayed up for 60 hours to finish writing one of his stories.

387. He was a ghost writer for Harry Houdini.

388. Although trolls are quite commonplace on YouTube, Lovecraft was a master troll and wrote countless critiques for other writers' works. He even wrote poems about how much he hated the work of the writer, Fred Jackson. He wasn't even subtle. The first two lines of this poem read,
"What vig'rous protests now assail my eyes?
See Jackson's satellites in anger rise!"

389. Lovecraft adored cats and said they had "superior imaginative inner life." He thought dogs were "pitiful" since they relied on their owners.

390. Although Lovecraft is one of the most influential horror writers, his work only become popular after he died. He died penniless at the age of 46.

Hans Christian Andersen

1343 – 1400

Written Work
The Little Mermaid (1837)
The Ugly Duckling (1843)
The Emperor's New Clothes (1837)
The Princess and the Pea (1835)

391. Hans Christian Andersen was born in Funen, Denmark.

392. He had a natural talent for cutting paper into intricate shapes such as a vase with flowers or a woman playing the bagpipes.

393. He wrote The Snow Queen, which inspired the film, Frozen. However, Andersen's version has next to nothing in common with the Disney movie.

394. It's easy to assume The Ugly Duckling is an allegory for Andersen's own life since he was incredibly thin and gangly, which led to him being bullied relentlessly. Andersen was mocked so often, he suffered from depression.

    But there's another theory about The Ugly Duckling. In the end, the duckling learns he is really a swan whose egg rolled into a duck's nest.

    Although Andersen lived in poverty, he was rumoured to be the illegitimate son of the prince of Denmark. So the theory suggests that Andersen was a "noble swan," not ""an ordinary duck."

395. His father introduced Andersen to 1001 Arabian Nights. It was this book that inspired Hans to be a writer.

396. Originally, he wanted to be an actor.

397. While visiting England in 1847, Andersen met his favourite writer, Charles Dickens. The pair admired each other's' works since their writings revolve around the difficulties that the underclass deal with.

    Ten years later, Andersen met Dickens' family at their home. With little explanation, Andersen decided to stay at Dickens' home for five weeks, much to the annoyance of Dicken's family. After Andersen was forced to leave, Dickens never spoke to him again. Although Andersen wrote to Dickens many times, Dickens never wrote back, much to Andersen's confusion.

398. Although Andersen wrote passionate love letters to many men and women, he was terrified of nudity and so, didn't have sexual relations with anyone.

399. Andersen's dyslexia was so bad, he never learned to spell properly. The first draft of his books were riddled with basic spelling mistakes.

400. He died of liver cancer at the age of 70.

Harper Lee

1926 - 2016

Written Work
To Kill a Mockingbird (1960)

401. Nelle Harper Lee published To Kill a Mockingbird in 1960. It won a Pulitzer Prize the following year.

402. She was best friends with Truman Capote when she was a child. She was played by Sandra Bullock in the film, Capote.

403. A million copies of To Kill a Mockingbird are sold every year.

404. To Kill a Mockingbird was adapted into a film in 1962. It won three Oscars and is considered to be one of the best films ever made.

405. Lee's mother was mentally unstable and probably suffered from undiagnosed bipolar.

406. British librarians did a poll to find the book that everyone should read before they die. To Kill a Mockingbird received the top spot. The Bible came in at #2.

407. She received the Presidential Medal of Freedom in 2007.

408. To Kill a Mockingbird had a sequel called Go Set a Watchman in 2015. Weirdly, it was the original draft of To Kill a Mockingbird. They are the only two books she ever wrote.

The title, "Go Set a Watchman" comes from the Biblical quote, Isaiah 21:6, "For thus hath the Lord said unto me, Go, set a watchman, let him declare what he seeth." The book was met with mixed reviews.

409. Go Set a Watchman is set 20 years after the original novel.

410. While writing to Kill a Mockingbird, Lee got so frustrated, she threw the manuscript out of the window. After her editor told Lee to get a grip, she ran out into the snow to pick up every page of her work.

Herman Melville

1819 - 1891

Written Work
Moby Dick (1851)

411. Herman Melville only made $3,000 from his book, Moby Dick. It didn't become popular for almost a century.

412. The coffee brand, Starbucks, is named after a character from Moby Dick.

413. In 2010, a new whale was discovered. In honor of Melville, it was nicknamed Livyatan melvillei.

414. The author of The Scarlet Letter, Nathaniel Hawthorne, believed that Moby Dick was "an epic worthy of Homer. It will be America's epic."

415. Melville wrote letters to Nathaniel Hawthorne that heavily imply that he was in love with Hawthorne. He wrote, "Your heart beats in my ribs and mine in yours. When come you, Hawthorne? By what right do you drink from my flagon of life? And when I put it to my lips – lo, they are yours and not mine." Melville wrote a letter to a friend reading, "Hawthorne has dropped germanous seeds into my soul. He expands and deepens down, the more I contemplate him; and further and further, shoots his strong New England roots in the hot soil of my Southern soul."

416. He wrote 11 novels in his lifetime. All his work was criticized while he was alive except for his debut book, Typee, which is now forgotten.

417. The musician, Richard Melville Hall, is related to Melville. If you don't recognise Richard Melville Hall's name, you probably know his stage name, Moby. Richard Hall took the name, Moby, from Herman Melville's greatest novel, Moby Dick. Speaking of which…

418. Moby Dick was based on a real whale called Mocha Dick. Mocha was an albino whale that intentionally knocked into ships near Chile in 1820. When Mocha blew his spout, it sounded like a roar. This description was incorporated into the Moby Dick novel. Mocha Dick inspired a 2015 film called In the Heart of the Sea. In the film, Melville is played by Ben Whishaw.

419. Melville died from a heart attack at the age of 72.

420. When he died, only one newspaper mentioned him and he was called "Henry Melville." He was referred to as "a forgotten author."

Homer

900 BC (Approx.) – 800 BC (Approx.)

Written Work
The Iliad (860 BC Approx.)
The Odyssey (850 Approx.)

421. Scholars have suggested that Homer may not have existed. Nobody knows anything about his life, his hometown, his date of birth, his family, or even his surname.

422. He was supposedly born blind.

423. If Homer existed, it's likely that the people he told his stories to wrote them down and tweaked them over the decades, maybe even centuries.

424. Some historians believe the name, "Homer" is a pseudonym for many authors over the years.

425. The Iliad was the first book to describe a mullet. It was referring to the appearance of a warrior tribe.

426. Seven towns claim to be the hometown of Homer including Ithaca and Chios. Some scholars suggested he was from Ionia, which now is in Turkey.

427. Homer is regarded as the first epic poet and his work is considered to be Europe's first known literature.

428. If you ask anyone what the most iconic moment in The Iliad or The Odyssey is, they will probably refer to the Wooden Horse of Troy. However, the Wooden Horse isn't mentioned in The Iliad and it's only briefly mentioned in The Odyssey. The first time the Wooden

Horse was written about in detail was in The Aeneid, which was written by Virgil between 29-19 BC.

429. According to the Ancient Greek novelist, Lucian, Homer was really a Babylonian called Tigranes. He was taken hostage by the Greeks and referred to as "homeros," which means "hostage." Since Lucian was a known satirist, it's safe to assume he was joking.

430. In Plato's work, Republics, he refers to Homer as the leader of Greek culture. Plato was born about 400 years after Homer's time.

Hunter S. Thompson

1938 - 2005

Written Work
Hell's Angels (1967)
The Rum Diary (1998)
Fear and Loathing in Las Vegas (1971)

431. Hunter Stockton Thompson accidentally shot his assistant with a shotgun while he was trying to scare a bear that was on his property.

432. He was nicknamed Dr. Gonzo due to popularizing Gonzo journalism. This is when a journalist writes a story without any objectivity. Gonzo journalists become a part of the story they are covering. Thompson's book, Hell's Angels, is based on his experience living with the famous biker gang for over a year.

433. The Rum Diary was written in the early 1960s but it wasn't published until 1998. It revolves around Thompson's experience as a journalist in Puerto Rico. The manuscript was discovered by Johnny Depp. Depp went on to star in the 2011 film, The Rum Diary.

434. Thompson was the main inspiration for the character, Spider Jerusalem, in the graphic novel, Transmetropolitan. The story revolves around the last non-corrupt journalist in 23rd century America revealing the corruption of the US government. And there are aliens. And two-headed cats. It's a fine read.

435. Thompson pranked Jack Nicholson on his birthday by shining a spotlight on his house while blasting out a recording of a pig being eaten by bears. Thompson left an elk's heart on Nicholson's front door and fired a

pistol in the air. Nicholson hid in the basement with his two daughters.

436. Johnny Depp plays Raoul Duke in the film, Fear and Loathing in Las Vegas. The character is based on Hunter S. Thompson. Thompson cameos in one scene. When Johnny Depp's character is stumbling through a club while on drugs, he sees Thompson and says, "There I was...mother of God, there I am!"

437. When Ernest Hemingway died, Thompson visited Hemingway's retreat to write an article dedicate to the legendary writer. After Thompson wrote the piece, he stole a pair of elk horns from Hemingway's cabin.

438. Actor, Don Johnson, asked Thompson the philosophical question, "What is the sound of one hand clapping?" Thompson answered by slapping Johnson in the face.

439. He wrote rejection letters while he worked for Rolling Stone magazine.
    When Anthony Burgess sent a novella to Rolling Stone, Thompson sent him a reply reading, "Herr Wenner has forwarded your useless letter from Rome to the National Affairs Desk for my examination and/or reply.
    Unfortunately, we have no International Gibberish Desk, or it would have ended up there.
    Do you take us for a gang of brainless lizards? Rich hoodlums? Dilettante thugs?
    The time has come & gone when cheapjack scum like you can get away with the kind of scams you got rich from in the past.
    Get your worthless ass out of the piazza and back to the typewriter."
    Luckily, Burgess ignored Thompson's insanity and

continued writing. He is best known for writing A Clockwork Orange.

You might be wondering why Thompson had such a personal hatred for Burgess.

He didn't. Thompson was like this with everybody. He also had disdain for Tom Wolfe, who is best known for writing The Bonfire of the Vanities. Thompson called Wolfe a "thieving pile of albino warts," "worthless scumsucker "a filthy swine" who will "have your goddamn femurs ground into bone splinters."

440. He shot himself dead in 2005. His ashes were shot from a cannon.

Isaac Asimov

1920 - 1992

Written Work
Foundation Series (1942-1993)
Galactic Empire Series (1945-1951)
Robot Series (1950-1985)

441. Isaac Asmiov's (born as Isaak Judah Ozimov) was born in Petrovichi in Russia (which was known as the Russian Soviet Federative Socialist Republic at the time.) He moved to the US at a very early age and didn't speak Russian.

442. He liked confined spaces and worked in windowless rooms.

443. It is unclear what day, month, or year Asimov was born in.

444. He was scared of flying and only flew twice in his entire life.

445. Asimov is famous for his Robot Series where he concocted The Three Laws of Robotics. This concept has been adapted into other stories and films such as Robocop. His book, I, Robot, was adapted into a 2004 film starring Will Smith. His story, Bicentennial Man, was adapted into a film with Robin Williams playing the main role.

446. His pride and joy was the Foundation series. It beat The Lord of the Rings for the Hugo award in 1966.

447. He was the first science-fiction writer to headline his own magazine.

448. He was a member of the largest IQ society in the world, Mensa.

449. He wrote over 500 books. Because of this, he was nicknamed The Human Typewriter.

450. He suffered a heart attack in 1977 and underwent a triple bypass operation in 1983. Many sources say he died in 1992 from kidney failure. However, it was later unveiled that Asimov contracted HIV during a blood transfusion during his operation. He died of AIDS.

JD Salinger

1919 - 2010

Written Work
The Catcher in the Rye (1951)

451. Jerome David Salinger wrote most of his work in a concrete bunker that his family were not allowed to enter.

452. Salinger was only 22 when he was sent out to fight in World War II. While he was away, his 16-year-old girlfriend, Oona, left him for a 52-year-old, Charlie Chaplin. Chaplin married Oona and stayed with her until his death.

453. He suffered from post-traumatic stress disorder after WWII.

454. His novel, Catcher in the Rye, is often regarded as "the Best Novel That Has Never Been Adapted Into a Film."

455. JD Salinger said that he would only allow The Catcher in the Rye to be made into a film if he played the lead character, Holden. This didn't make any sense since Holden is a teenager and Salinger was 32 when he wrote it.

456. He despised all forms of technology.

457. Mark David Chapman was obsessed with The Catcher in the Rye and was reading the book just before he shot John Lennon dead.

458. Although he's mainly known for writing The Catcher in the Rye, Salinger wrote many other stories including Nine Stories and Franny and Zooey.

459. A neighbour once went over to Salinger's house and asked him if he would help fund a charity. Salinger pointed a gun at his neighbour and told him to go away.

460. His will stipulates that none of his work can be adapted into Hollywood films.

JK Rowling

1965 -

Written Work
The Harry Potter Series (1997-2007)

461. Joanne Rowling was born in Yate, Gloucestershire, in England.

462. While she was teaching English in Portugal, she met Jorge Arantes. They married in 1992 and had one child. They divorced in 1995. She married Neil Murray in 2001 and had two daughters and a son.

463. The Harry Potter series were the most banned books of the century in the US.

464. JK Rowling wrote the final chapter of the last Harry Potter book in 1990, seven years before the release of the first book.

465. Harry Potter and the Philosopher's Stone was accepted by a publishing house called Bloomsbury. The chairman of Bloomsbury allowed his eight-year-old niece, Alice, to read the first chapter of the book. When she demanded to know what happened next, Bloomsbury agreed to publish the story.

466. It's common knowledge that Rowling's first novel was turned down by 13 different publishing houses. The reason it was rejected was because it was twice as long as the average children's novel.

467. The main female character in the Harry Potter series is Hermione. If the female character had a common name like Laura, JK Rowling was worried that girls

called Laura would be made fun of. This is why she chose the unusual name, Hermione.

468. Harry Potter and the Philosopher's Stone has sold over 107 million copies, making it the fifth most successful novel of all time.

469. Although many people believe Rowling is a billionaire, she was knocked off the Forbes billionaire list in 2012 because she gives so much money to charity. She is currently worth approximately $910 million.

470. When JK Rowling was accepted by Bloomsbury, they gave her a $2,400 advance. They told her to get a day job as people can't rely on the income earned from maintain from selling children's books.
    They can.

JM Barrie

1860 - 1937

Written Work
Peter Pan or The Boy Who Never Grew Up (1904)

471. James Matthew Barrie had a tragic upbringing. When his brother, David, died in an ice-skating accident, his mother became so traumatised that she neglected Barrie.

    Barrie dressed up as his deceased brother to get his mother's attention.

    Although this worked for a while, Barrie eventually outgrew his brother's clothes.

    Barrie wanted to remain young forever so he could keep playing the role of David to appease his mother. This obsession drove him to write the play, Peter Pan.

472. Barrie had many connections with other writers. He played cricket with Arthur Conan Doyle, was a neighbour of George Bernard Shaw, and was friends with HG Wells.

473. After his friends, Arthur and Sylvia Llewelyn-Davies died, Barrie adopted their five children.

474. Although Barrie was married for 15 years, he never had sex with his wife.

475. Most of Barrie's plays didn't do well in theatres and he never wrote a play that reached the success of Peter Pan. In his own words, "some of my plays peter out, others pan out."

476. JM Barrie is responsible for naming the Quality Street chocolate brand.

477. The Peter Pan character first appeared in one chapter in Barrie's 1902 novel, The Little White Bird.

478. Captain Hook is based on a reverend that Barrie knew called John Maher who had a hook for a hand.

479. In Peter Pan, children can fly if they think of a happy memory. Many children who saw or read the play injured themselves by jumping off high buildings in an attempt to fly. Barrie had to add in a line stating that a person can only fly if he thinks of a happy memory AND he is covered in fairy dust.

480. Barrie's manager, Charles Frohman, died during World War I when the Germans sank his ship, the Lusitania. After the ship was torpedoed, he was offered a seat on a lifeboat. He gave up his spot on the boat and said, "Why fear death? It is the most beautiful adventure that life gives us." This is a paraphrase from Peter Pan when the titular character states "to die would be a great adventure."

JRR Tolkien

1892 - 1973

Written Work
The Hobbit (1937)
The Lord of the Rings (1954-1955)

481. His full name is John Ronald Reuel Tolkien. "Tolkien" means "foolhardy."

482. Tolkien was a professor of linguistics at Oxford University. While grading papers, he spontaneously wrote, "In a hole in the ground there lived a hobbit." He didn't know what a hobbit was supposed to be. He simply liked the sound of the word.
    Tolkien believed he coined the word, hobbit, and said it meant "hole-builder." However, the word has existed since the 19th century and references a type of hobgoblin. Nowadays, it's used to reference a person of diminutive stature.

483. JRR Tolkien first used the word "tween" in The Lord of the Rings: The Fellowship of the Ring to describe the character, Frodo.

484. According to Tolkien, Samwise is the true hero of The Lord of the Rings since he is the only person who voluntarily surrenders the Ring. Not only that, he does it without hesitation.

485. In the first edition of The Hobbit, it never describes how large Gollum is. Some illustrated copies of the book show Gollum being over 10ft tall. This was changed in later editions because it is revealed in The Lord of the Rings that Gollum is a hobbit, which would make him about 3ft tall.

486. Tolkien was kidnapped as a toddler for one day. He was returned unharmed.

487. Although The Hobbit was loved when it was released, The Lord of the Rings was criticised for being too long and confusing. Since it didn't sell well, Tolkien's publisher split the book into three novels to make more cash. Tolkien hated this idea as he believed the novel was a self-contained story and buying one book meant people would be only reading one-third of the tale. He was angry that the third part was called The Return of the King because it spoilt the ending. He wanted the third part to be called The War of the Ring but his publisher refused.

488. Although The Lord of the Rings is now considered to be the superior novel, The Hobbit is more successful, selling over 100 million copies.

489. Tolkien wrote 13 pages of a sequel to The Lord of the Rings. It was set a century after the events of the previous story and revolved around a "secret Satanistic religion."

490. Tolkien was a philologist, which meant that he studied the history of languages. In fact, Tolkien was such an expert with languages that he was one of the translators of the Jerusalem Bible.

James Joyce

1882 - 1941

Written Work
Ulysses (1922)
Dubliners (1914)
Finnegan's Wake (1939)
A Portrait of the Artist as a Young Man (1916)

491. James Augustine Aloysius Joyce was born in Dublin, Ireland.

492. James Joyce coined the word "quark" in his novel, Finnegan's Wake.

493. James Joyce believed his greatest work was his 1900 play, A Brilliant Career. He dedicated the story to his own soul. Sadly, Joyce grew paranoid that he would be accused of plagiarism since many characters and incidents in the story are based on people he knew in real life. Joyce destroyed the play two years later. To date, only two pages of it still exist.

494. Joyce developed cynophobia (fear of canines) after he was attacked by a dog when he was five years old. Joyce also suffered from keraunophobia (fear of lightning) after his aunt told Joyce that thunder was the sound of God's wrath.

495. During the outbreak of World War I, Joyce moved to neutral Switzerland.

496. British war censors thought the writing style in Ulysses was so bizarre, some of them worried it was a spy code.

497. A first edition of Ulysses was sold in 2009 for £275,000.

498. Although Ulysses was published in 1922, it wasn't available in the UK until 1936.

499. Joyce's work was banned in China from 1945-1976 for being too decadent. When his books were released in China, they became incredibly successful. In fact, Ulysses became a #1 best seller in China in 2013.

500. Although Ulysses is his Joyce's most famous book, he was almost blind when he wrote it. Although he had glasses, his doctor told Joyce not to wear them, believing that his eyes would naturally get stronger...which they didn't. Although he had ten optic operations, Joyce was almost sightless in the last 20 years of his life. Because Joyce couldn't see his own writing when he used an ordinary pencil, he wrote Ulysses in huge letters with a red crayon. You might think, "How could he possibly write blindly without some spelling errors?" Well, there were a few. When he wrote words like "devlinsfirst" and "goragorridgeorballyedpuhkalsom," many of his readers assumed Joyce was creating words, as John Milton or William Shakespeare did. However, these "words" are simply spelling mistakes that nobody corrected because...well, who corrects a blind guy?

Jane Austen

1775 - 1817

Written Work
Sense and Sensibility (1811)
Pride and Prejudice (1813)
Emma (1815)

501. Jane Austen almost died as a child from typhus.

502. She quit school when she was only ten years old. Austen said she was "the most unlearned and uninformed female who ever dared to be an authoress."

503. The first book she wrote was Love and Friendship. She misspelt the title as "Love and Freindship."

504. She wrote Pride and Prejudice, Northanger Abbey, and Sense and Sensibility before she was 23 years old. However, Sense and Sensibility wasn't published until 1811 when she was 35. Pride and Prejudice was published in 1813 and Northanger Abbey wasn't published until 1818. This means that her last novel was published a year after Austen died.

505. Charlotte Bronte didn't think much of Austen's work and called her "a very incomplete and rather insensible woman." She wasn't the only one who wasn't a fan. Mark Twain HATED her work. He once said, "Every time I read Pride and Prejudice, I want to dig her up and beat her over the skull with her own shin bone!"

506. Her books were published anonymously. Originally, Sense and Sensibility was said to be written "By A Lady." Pride and Prejudice was said to be written "By the Author of Sense and Sensibility."

507. She was engaged to Harris Biggs Wither for one day. After sleeping on it, Austen changed her mind and rejected him. Austen never married.

508. She wasn't famous during her lifetime. Over half a century after she died, Austen became popular when her nephew, JE Austen-Leigh, released her biography. She was only perceived as one of the greatest writers ever after Mary Lascelles wrote Jane Austen and Her Art in the 1940s.

509. She only mentioned three people in her will. Most of her family were left nothing.

510. On Austen's death bed, her attendant asked her if she needed anything. She said, "Nothing but death." She died when she was only 41.

Although Austen was originally reported to have died from Addison's disease, it's more likely she died from Hodgkin's lymphoma.

Jean-Paul Sartre

1749 - 1832

Written Work
Existentialism is a Humanism (1946)
Dirty Hands (1948)

511. Jean-Paul Charles-Aymard Sartre was born in Paris, France.

512. He had an Algerian mistress called Arlette Elkaim. She eventually became his adopted daughter.

513. Sartre suffered horrific exotropia, which meant his eyes deviated outward. It was so bad, he regularly lost his balance.

514. He had a cat called Nothing.

515. He was only 5ft tall.

516. He popularised the concept of existentialism, atheism, and meta-physics.

517. He was awarded the Nobel Prize in 1964 but he turned it down because he didn't "want to be an institution." He is one of two writers to have declined to accept a Nobel Prize.

518. His most famous quote was, "Hell is other people."

519. He was a meteorologist for the French military during WWII. Sartre was captured by the Nazis a year later and held as a prisoner of war for nine months.

520. 50,000 people attended his funeral.

Johann Wolfgang von Goethe

1749 - 1832

Written Work
Faust (1790-1831)
The Sorrows of Young Werther (1774-1787)

521. Goethe is considered to be Germany's greatest poet and playwright.

522. He is best known for writing Faust, which revolves around a scholar who makes a pact with the Devil in exchange for power and knowledge. It took him over 50 years to write the story. He died very soon after completing it.

523. He was petrified of dogs.

524. He spoke many languages from a young age including Latin, Greek, French, Italian, English, and Hebrew.

525. His first story was in English even though his first language was German.

526. His literary work influenced the Swiss psychoanalyst, Carl Jung.

527. He had an IQ of 210.

528. He famously said, "Nothing shows a man's character more than what he laughs at."

529. His novel, Sorrows of Young Werther, concludes with the titular character shooting himself in the head after growing frustrated in a doomed relationship.

Many readers were so gripped by Werther's struggle, there were reports of young people taking their own lives in the same manner as Werther. These suicides got so out of hand, that the book had to be banned in several countries.

530. He died at the age of 82 from a heart attack.

John Milton

1608 - 1674

Written Work
Paradise Lost (1667)
Poetical Works (1752-1761)

531. Milton is best known for writing the epic poem, Paradise Lost. It is often regarded as the greatest English poem. It tells the story of how Lucifer fell from Heaven and sought revenge upon God. Lucifer takes on the form of a snake and enters the Garden of Eden and convinces Adam and Eve to eat from the Tree of Knowledge, which causes them to experience Original Sin.

    Milton created several concepts in Paradise Lost that many Christians falsely believe are in the Bible. In the Bible, it never states angels have two wings or haloes. The Bible never mentions that angels pluck harps. These ideas came from Paradise Lost. In the Biblical account of Genesis, a snake encourages Adam and Eve to eat from the Tree of Knowledge. However, it is never stated in the Bible that this snake is Satan.

532. Although William Shakespeare is believed to be the writer who coined more English words than anyone else, this isn't true. Shakespeare coined more English phrases than anyone else, with over 2,000 to his credit. However, he only concocted 229 words. Milton, on the other hand, coined 630 words. Milton came up with the words – awe-struck, cooking, criticize, damp, debauchery, disregard, exhilarating, extravagance, incidental, stunning, terrific, unconvincing, undesirable, fragrance, earth-shaking, and pandemonium. He was the first person to use the word "space" to refer to "outer space." Also, he coined the phrase "by hook or by

crook."

533. His grandfather was a composer for Queen Elizabeth I.

534. He strongly considered becoming a priest.

535. Milton was married three times. He had four children with his first wife, Mary Powell, until she died in 1652. He had one child with his second wife, Katherine Woodcock, until she died in 1658. He married Elizabeth Minshull in 1663. They were together until Milton died from gout in 1674.

536. He was blind by the time Paradise Lost was published.

537. He used to be a huge advocate of Oliver Cromwell. When he renounced Cromwell, Milton was sentenced to death until King Charles decided to spare him.

538. William Lauder accused Milton of plagiarising Paradise Lost from other writings. It was later unveiled that Lauder had inserted lines from Paradise Lost into other poems because he was jealous of Milton's success.

539. He met Galileo in 1638. Some historians have suggested that their meeting influenced Milton's description of the Heavens in Paradise Lost.

540. George Cudmore was hanged after he was found guilty of hanging his wife. Now, you might be asking, "What does this have to do with John Milton?"
    Well, a bookkeeper came into possession of Cudmore's skin and used it to bind the 1852 edition of Milton's book, Poetical Works. This means that one of Milton's books is bound in the skin of a murderer.

John Steinbeck

1902 - 1968

Written Work
Of Mice and Men (1937)
The Grapes of Wrath (1939)
East of Eden (1952)

541. John Ernst Steinbeck's puppy ate half of the manuscript for his novel, Of Mice and Men.

542. Of Mice and Men was nearly called Something That Happened.

543. His novel, The Grapes of Wrath revolves around a family forced out of their home during the Great Depression. It won Steinbeck a Pulitzer Prize in 1939 and was the most popular book of the year. It won a Nobel Prize in 1962.

544. He was the first person to refer to Route 66 as The Mother Road.

545. There's a rumor that The Grapes of Wrath title was mistranslated as The Angry Raisins in Japan but this is untrue.

546. He was nominated for an Oscar for writing the stories for three films – Lifeboat, A Medal for Benn, and Viva Zapata!

547. He would wear his pencils down so much while writing, he used up to 60 pencils a day. Steinbeck went through 300 pencils to write East of Eden.

548. Although The Grapes of Wrath is hailed as a masterpiece for showing daily life in America during the Great Depression, some people despised it because it made Americans look weak. The book was dubbed "a pack of lies" and Steinbeck was accused of being a Communist. The book was banned in certain places in the US and burned in his own hometown.

549. He died of heart disease at the age of 66.

550. He is related to Barack Obama.

Jonathan Swift

1667 - 1745

Written Work
Gulliver's Travels (1726)

551. Jonathan Swift was born in Dublin in the Kingdom of Ireland (now known as the Republic of Ireland.)

552. Jonathan Swift coined the word, "yahoo," in his novel, Gulliver's Travels. The word was used to describe a group of mindless savages.

    He also created the name, Vanessa, and coined the phrase, "sweetness and light."

553. His cousin was the English poet, John Dryden.

554. Many people know Gulliver's Travels as the story of a man who discovers the land of Lilliput which is populated by people who are only six-inches tall. However, this is only a small part of the story. After he leaves Lilliput, he goes to the land of the giants, Brobdingnag. Although the giants look intimidating, they have no concept of war or poverty.

    Gulliver then ventures to the floating island of Laputa where the inhabitants use music and art for nonsensical reasons.

    He lands in Balnibarbi where the citizens are incapable of using science correctly.

    Gulliver sets sail to Glubbdubdrib, where he meets the ghosts of historical figures.

    He heads to Luggnagg where he meets immortal beings called Strudbrugs.

    Lastly, he makes his way to the Land of the Houyhnhnms, which is populated by savages called Yahoos and talking horses called Houyhnhnms. When he returns home, he cannot adapt to life and goes completely insane.

555. In Gulliver's Travels, the titular character visits the floating island of Laputa. The scientists tell Gulliver that they have made huge discoveries throughout the cosmos. They were the first to learn that Mars had two moons. This novel was written over 150 years before Mars' moons, Deimos and Phobos, were discovered. Stranger still, Swift describes the moons' patterns with astounding accuracy. To commemorate Swift, NASA named a crater on Deimos after the writer.

556. Although he is immortalised for his work on Gulliver's Travels, he wrote other stories including A Tale of a Tub, Drapier's Letters, and A Modest Proposal.

557. He was known for his deadpan ironic satirical writing style, especially in Gulliver's Travels. His style is so distinctive, any writer who wrote in a similar manner would be referred to as Swiftian.

558. He used to be a vicar.

559. Gulliver's Travels was originally called Travels into Several Remote Nations of the World. In Four Parts. By Lemuel Gulliver, First a Surgeon, and then a Captain of Several Ships. That is not a joke.

560. According to his friends, Swift went mad in the last seven years of his life. When he was 74, he had an episode (possibly a stroke,) which left him unstable and violent. He suffered horrific inflammations on his face near the end of his life. His eye swelled to the size of an egg and left him so irascible, five attendants had to pin him down as he desperately tried to tear his own eye out. He died in 1745 at the age of 77.

Joseph Conrad

1857 - 1924

Written Work
Heart of Darkness (1899)
Nostromo (1904)

561. His real name is Jozef Teodor Konrad Korzeniowski.

562. Conrad was in such heavy debt when he was 21, he shot himself in the chest in an attempted suicide. Miraculously, he survived for another 46 years.

563. Conrad was born in Poland. He was granted British nationality in 1886.

564. He spoke Russian, Polish, and French fluently. Conrad couldn't speak English well until he was in his 20s. Conrad picked up the language by listening to sailors upon his many voyages. Over time, he became an excellent English speaker.

565. His book, Heart of Darkness, was adapted into the film, Apocalypse Now, which is often considered to be the greatest war film ever. Weirdly, Conrad wrote the book in English, even though that was his third language. He believed the Polish language wasn't strong enough to convey the most savage side of war. Conrad believed that English was the only language visceral enough to bring his story to life.

566. Conrad sailed to South America, Malay States, Borneo, Siam, Australia, and many other places. Because of his fondness for sailing, many of Conrad's stories take place by the sea.

567. Conrad's first novel was Almayer Folly. He was 37 when it was published.

568. Although Conrad didn't read reviews of his work, he measured them with a ruler. The longer the review was, the happier he felt.

569. In Heart of Darkness, a sailor called Marlow explores Africa during its British colonization. Although many incidents in the book are based on Conrad's experience while he was sailing, most critics stated that the book oversimplified African life. One of the biggest critics of Conrad's work was the renowned Nigerian author, Chinua Achebe, who is best known for writing Things Fall Apart. He said that Conrad is "blinkered with xenophobia" which caused him to write "an offensive and deplorable book."

570. Conrad died of a heart attack at the age of 66.

Jules Verne

1828 - 1905

Written Work
Twenty Thousand Leagues Under the Sea (1870)
The Mysterious Island (1874)
Journey to the Centre of the Earth (1864)
Around the World in Eighty Days (18703)
From the Earth to the Moon (1865)

571. Jules Gabriel Verne was born in Nantes in France.

572. When Verne was 11, he tried to travel to the Indies as a cabin boy on a ship. His father got to the ship on time before it set sail, stopping Verne's journey.

573. He studied law in Paris. After a blind geographer called Jacques Arago introduced Verne to literature, he gave up law and decided to become a novelist, much to his father's dismay.

574. He didn't like HG Wells' writing because it was too unrealistic. (Reminder – Verne wrote a book where men venture to the centre of the Earth where they meet mammoths and 12ft tall prehistoric men.)

575. Verne bought his own ship and travelled around the world with his wife for many years.

576. His favourite nephew, Gaston, suffered from mental illness. During one of his episodes, Gaston shot Verne in the shin, which left Verne in pain for the rest of his life. Gaston was sent to a mental institution.

577. He famously said, "Anything one man can imagine, other men can make real."

578.   He is nicknamed The Father of Science Fiction.

579.   He is the most translated author in the world apart from Agatha Christie.

580.   In 1863, Jules Verne wrote Paris in the 20th Century. This story described a world with submarines, feminism, glass skyscrapers, rising illegitimate births, and technology that allowed mankind to walk on the Moon. Weirdly, the spaceship in the book takes off from Florida just like the Apollo 11 ship did in 1969. Verne also described how the astronauts felt weightless as they ascended from Earth. At the time of this book's publication, astronomers didn't know that space travel could alter an astronaut's gravity. Verne's publisher rejected the story because it was too unrealistic. Verne locked it away in a safe until it was discovered by his great-grandson in 1989.

Kenneth Grahame

1859 - 1932

Written Work
The Wind in the Willows (1908)

581. Kenneth Grahame was born in Edinburgh in Scotland.

582. Grahame suffered from scarlet fever when he was a child. This left Grahame in a fragile state for the rest of his life.

583. His father was a raging alcoholic. When Grahame's mother died when he was five, he and his three siblings, Willie, Helen, and Roland, were sent to live with their grandmother.

584. Grahame was the captain of his football team while in high school.

585. Grahame used to be the Secretary of the Bank of England. He quit after a robber shot at him three times. Luckily, Grahame wasn't injured.

586. His children's book, The Reluctant Dragon, was published in 1898. He published The Wind in the Willows ten years later. Both stories were adapted into Disney films in the 1940s.

587. He retired immediately after releasing The Wind in the Willows.

588. President Theodore Roosevelt loved The Wind in the Willows so much, he personally met Grahame when he visited Oxford.

589. He married Elspeth Thompson in 1899. They had one son called Alastair. Alastair was born blind and suffered from health problems over his entire life. He died when he was only 20 years old.

590. Grahame came up with The Wind in the Willows as a bedtime story for his son.

Kurt Vonnegut

1922 - 2007

Written Work
Slaughterhouse-Five (1969)

591. When Vonnegut was 22, he returned home on Mother's Day to find his mother had taken her own life by overdosing on sleeping pills.

592. During WWII, Vonnegut was captured by the Nazis and held at a POW camp. The camp used to be an abattoir and was known as Slaughterhouse-Five. This inspired him to write his masterpiece, Slaughterhouse-Five.

593. Vonnegut became so depressed after writing Slaughterhouse-Five, that he stopped writing novels for years. Vonnegut's depression got so bad, he tried to take his own life in 1984.

594. Vonnegut tried to sue the cigarette group, Pall Mall, for false advertising. He had been smoking Pall Mall cigs for 13 years and complained that he was still not dead even though the company advertised that they kill people. He died one year later.

595. Vonnegut was a passionate atheist and argued with his wife after she converted to Christianity.

596. Vonnegut was an excellent artist. He painted illustrations for his books on silk-screen prints.

597. Vonnegut wrote 14 novels, 81 articles, 16 collections, a poem, seven plays, and 123 stories.

598. Vonnegut never studied writing.

599. His books, Mother Night and Breakfast of Champions, were adapted into films. He cameoed in both films.

600. He passed away in 2007 at the age of 84. Three of his books were published after his death – Armageddon in Retrospect was released in 2008, Look at the Birdie in 2009, and While Mortals Sleep in 2011.

L. Frank Baum

1856 - 1919

Written Work
The Wonderful Wizard of Oz (1900)

601. Lyman Frank Baum was a huge advocate of the woman's suffragette movement, which was rare for his time. In fact, The Wonderful Wizard of Oz had many feminist themes that were removed from the film adaptation.

602. He was a chicken farmer, an actor, a store owner, a salesman, a newspaper editor, a fireworks seller, and a chandelier designer.

603. While on tour with his play, The Maid of Arran, Baum's own theatre burnt down. All the scripts were burnt in the fire.

604. Baum wrote the Wonderful Wizard of Oz in 1900. It sold out after two weeks and was a #1 best-selling book for two years. It had at least 17 sequels including The Marvellous Land of Oz, Queen Visitors form the Marvellous Land of Oz, The Woggle-Bug Book, Ozma of Oz, Dorothy and the Wizard of Oz, The Road to Oz, The Emerald City of Oz, The Patchwork Girl of Oz, Little Wizard Stories of Oz, Tik-Tok of Oz, The Scarecrow of Oz, Rinkitink in Oz, The Lost Princess of Oz, The Tin Woodman of Oz, and Glinda of Oz. Three of them were published posthumously.

605. In The Wonderful Wizard of Oz, the Tin Woodsman used to be a real man. A witch used magic on his axe so he kept cutting himself. Every time he lost a limb, he had a tinsmith replace it with tin. Over time, he had

every part of his body replaced with tin, including his head.

606. Baum was the seventh child of nine. Only five of his siblings lived to adulthood.

607. He was obsessed with stamp collecting and wrote a meticulous stamp-collecting guide.

608. Baum didn't like his first name and preferred to be called Frank.

609. He died after suffering a stroke when he was 62.

610. One of the jackets for the film, The Wizard of Oz, was bought at a second-hand store. By a complete coincidence, the jacket belonged to L. Frank Baum.

Leo Tolstoy

1828 - 1910

Written Work
War and Peace (1869)
Anna Karenina (1877)

611.   Count Lev Nikolayevich Tolstoy hated Shakespeare and said the plays were full of "irresistible repulsion and tedium."
   Many years later, Tolstoy decided to give Shakespeare another chance, believing he would appreciate the playwright's work more since he was older and wiser. After reading every single Shakespeare play, Tolstoy stated that he hated them even more. Tolstoy said he felt the same disdain but "with even greater force, the same feelings, this time, however, not of bewilderment, but of firm, indubitable conviction." He felt that holding Shakespeare in such high regard was "a great evil."

612.   Tolstoy gave away most of his money to charity. When he realised how much this annoyed his wife, Tolstoy donated his royalties to her. He wrote and illustrated a book of ABCs for peasant children since they couldn't afford to go to school.

613.   He and Sofya had 13 children. Only 10 lived to infancy.

614.   Tolstoy dropped out of university halfway through the course to start his career as a writer. The first thing he wrote was a biography called Boyhood.

615.   Tolstoy fought in the Crimean War from November 1854 to August 1855. During this time, he wrote

Boyhood, the second book in an autobiographical trilogy.

616. Tolstoy saw a public execution in Paris in 1857, which unsettled him for the rest of his life. He wrote about the experience in his third autobiographical book, Youth.

617. Because his books were so influential, the Russian secret police used to spy on Tolstoy.

618. He became incredibly religious in the last three decades of his life. Mahatma Gandhi said he was inspired by Tolstoy.

619. His two novels, Anna Karenina and War and Peace, are often considered to be the best novels ever written.

620. Tolstoy loved Around the World in 80 Days so much, he drew scenes from the story all the time.

Lewis Carroll

1832 - 1898

Written Work
Alice's Adventures in Wonderland (1865)
Through the Looking-Glass (1871)
Jabberwocky (1871)
The Hunting of the Snark (1876)

621. His real name was Charles Lutwidge Dodgson.

622. Through the Looking Glass was the first book to use the word "chortle."

623. He taught mathematics for 24 years. During his lifetime, mathematics evolved exponentially as lettered maths ($x + y = z$) and fractions bigger than the whole (10/6ths) became more commonplace. However, Carroll was a traditionalist and believed mathematics had stayed relatively the same for millennia and shouldn't be replaced with "absurd math." Although many people believe Alice's Adventures in Wonderland is an allusion to hallucinogenic drugs, Carrol wrote the story to show how stupid maths had become! Everything in Wonderland seems to be shrinking or growing because the world has no set-in-stone rules. This was an allusion to Carroll's belief that the mathematic world no longer had any grounding. To highlight this point even further, the most insane character, The Hatter, has a price tag on his hat that reads 10/6, which is obviously a fraction that is larger than a whole number.

624. Carroll was obsessed with looking at larvae through his microscope.

625. He was deaf in one ear for most of his life. He also suffered from chronic migraines, epilepsy, and stuttering.

626. He trained himself to write 20 words a minute and 12 pages in 150 minutes.

627. He wrote up to 2,000 letters a year. Sometimes, he wrote backwards just to annoy the person he was writing to.

628. The Dodo is a character in Alice's Adventures in Wonderland. This character is based on Lewis Carroll. Like Carroll, the Dodo has a stutter. When Carroll said his real surname, it sounded like "Dodogson."

629. The most famous adaptation of Alice's Adventures in Wonderland is the 1951 Disney film, Alice in Wonderland. There are several differences between the book and the film.

    First off, the film is based on the first two books in the Wonderland series, Alice's Adventures in Wonderland and Through the Looking Glass. The Doorknob is the only character in the film that wasn't in the original story. The Mad Hatter is simply called The Hatter in the book. Most of the animals in the book look realistic. Tweedledee and Tweedledum appear in Through the Looking Glass but are absent from the first book. Also, there is no reference in the books that the Tweedles are twins.

630. By the time Carroll died from pneumonia at the age of 65, Alice's Adventures in Wonderland was the most popular book in England.

Lord Byron

1788 - 1824

Written Work
Don Juan (1819)
Manfred (1817)

631. George Gordon Byron was 21 when he took his seat in The House of Lords.

632. When Lord Byron went to Cambridge, he wanted to bring his dog. He was told it was forbidden. To spite the college, he bought a bear and brought it to Cambridge.

633. John Keats despised Lord Byron. Keats once wrote a letter to his brother reading, "You speak of Lord Byron and me. There is this great difference between us. He described what he sees – I describe what I imagine – Mine is the hardest task."

634. His daughter, Ada Lovelace, was a maths prodigy and worked with Charles Babbage on the Analytical Engine. Some would consider this device to be the first computer. She personally created the first algorithm to be carried out by a machine.

635. Byron married Anna Milbank in 1815. Anna gave birth to Ada that same year. Anna took Ada and left Byron as his alcoholism worsened. He never saw Ada or Anna again.

636. Mary Shelley (who wrote Frankenstein) had her husband's heart stolen. I don't mean that figuratively. Leigh Hunt literally stole Percy Shelley's heart from his body. Byron convinced Hunt to return the heart to allow Shelley to grieve for her husband.

637. He had a collection of wine goblets that were made from skulls.

638. He supposedly had an affair with his half-sister.

639. Byron is seen as one of the most prolific figures of the Romantic Movement; an artistic, intellectual, and literacy movement in Europe during the 19th century.

640. He left England at 28, never to return. He died in Greece at the age of 36. He suffered from sepsis, which developed into a fatal fever. His body was returned to England where he was buried.

Louisa May Alcott

1832 - 1888

Written Work
Little Women (1868-1869)

641. Louisa May Alcott was the first person to use the abbreviation "co-ed" in the 1886 novel, Jo's Boys.

642. She wrote most of her early work under the name, Flora Fairfield.

643. Her most famous book was Little Women, which she wrote in 1868. It was semi-autobiographical and revolved around her impoverished childhood and her relationship with her sisters.

644. She worked as a nurse in Washington DC during the American Civil War.

645. Many people don't know that Little Women has several sequels. She published Good Wives in 1869, Little Men in 1871, and Jo's Boys in 1886.

646. Alcott never married.

647. She was addicted to opium for her entire adult life.

648. So what spurred Alcott to write Little Women? Was it her family? Her childhood? No. It was money. In her own words, "money is the means and the end of my mercenary existence." She didn't particularly like her stories and referred to Little Women as "moral pap for the young." She knew that she was perceived as a goody-two-shoes and needed to preserve this image to maintain her sales. As a result, she never claimed

ownership of her earlier work since it was much more...erotic than Little Women.

649.   She died from a stroke at the age of 55. Her father died two days earlier.

650.   She wrote The Inheritance in 1849. It wasn't published until 1997. This means that it wasn't published for almost 150 years after it was written.

Mark Twain

1835 - 1910

Written Work
Adventures of Huckleberry Finn (1884)
The Adventures of Tom Sawyer (1876)

651. His real name was Samuel Langhorne Clemens. Although he is better known as Mark Twain, he had many pseudonyms including Thomas Jefferson Snodgrass, Rambler, Sergeant Fathom, and Epaminondas Adrastus Blab.

652. Although Mark Twain didn't coin the term "hard-boiled" he was the first person to use it to describe a person. He also coined the word "bicentennial" and "blip."

653. He was friends with the inventor, Nikola Tesla.

654. Halley's Comet appeared on the day that Twain was born and died. Weirdly, he predicted this by saying, "I came in with Halley's Comet. It is coming again.... And I expect to go out with it. The Almighty has said, no doubt: 'Now here are these two unaccountable freaks; they came in together, they must go out together."

655. He famously said, "Politicians and diapers must be changed often, and for the same reason."

656. The quote, "Reports of my death have been heavily exaggerated" has been inaccurately associated with many famous figures. It was Mark Twain who said it first after he read his own obituary... on two different occasions.

657. He adored Joan of Arc and spent 12 years travelling through Europe to find as much information about her as possible. Twain eventually wrote a book about her called Personal Recollections of Joan of Arc, where he looks at her life from the viewpoint of a fictional servant called Sieur Louis de Conte.

658. In 1898, Mark Twain came up with the idea of a telelectroscope. He said this invention would have "the improved limitless-distance telephone as presently introduced, and the daily doings of the globe made visible to everybody, and audibly discussable too, by witnesses separated by any number of leagues. Day by day, and night by night, he called up one corner of the globe after another, and looked upon its life, and studied its strange sights, and spoke with its people, and realized that by grace of this marvelous instrument he was almost as free as the birds of the air."

This invention exists today. It's called the Internet.

659. Twain wrote 28 books. Four of them were published after his death.

660. Twain challenged a rival to a duel in 1864. Since Twain had no experience of shooting, he started to practice before the duel was scheduled. However, Twain was such a bad shot that he "couldn't shoot a barn door." When his rival sent spies to see how Twain was getting on with his shooting, Twain happened to shoot the head off a sparrow. The spies assumed Twain was a natural shot and told his rival to back down.

Mary Shelley

1797 - 1851

Written Work
Frankenstein: or, The Modern Prometheus (1818)

661. Her mother, Mary Wollstonecraft, was a pioneer of feminism. Wollstonecraft published her work, A Vindication of the Rights of Woman, in 1792 which protested against the subordination of women.

662. Mary Wollstonecraft died 11 days after giving birth to Mary Shelley. This gave Shelley the idea that creating life can also take life away. This concept became the basis of her story, Frankenstein.

663. In Frankenstein, the Monster is brought to life by transplanting organs from several bodies. This was a unique concept at the time since this book was written five years before the first organ transplant took place.

664. While pregnant, Shelley eloped with her husband, Percy, when she was only 16. Percy left his wife, Harriet, to be with Mary Shelley. Harriet committed suicide soon afterwards.

665. When her husband, Percy, drowned in a sailing accident, his body was burned on the beach. His friends were baffled to see that Percy's entire body burned except his heart.

666. After Frankenstein was written, many scientists truly believed that the dead would be re-animated in the not-too-distant future.

667. Frankenstein was published anonymously.

668. She concocted the basis of Frankenstein while at a dinner with Lord Byron.

669. Although Mary Shelley is known for writing Frankenstein, she also wrote short stories, children's books, and travelogues.

670. Mary Shelley died of brain cancer when she was 53.

Maya Angelou

1928 - 2014

Written Work
I Know Why the Caged Bird Sings (1969)
On the Pulse of Morning (1993)

671. Her real name is Marguerite Annie Johnson. Her brother, Bailey Jr, called her, Maya, which means "my sister."

672. She was abused by a man when she was only eight years old. The man was released from prison after one day only to be murdered on his release date. Angelou went mute for five years, believing that she was responsible for his death. During her five years of silence, she fell in love with stories and poems.

673. She worked with Martin Luther King Jr. during the Civil Rights Movement.

674. She was a professional calypso dancer in 1954 and 1955.

675. She was nominated for a Pulitzer Prize and received a Presidential Medal of Honour.

676. She was the first black female in San Francisco to be a streetcar conductor. She was 20th Century Fox's first black female producer and director. Also, her story, Georgia, Georgia, was the first production to be written by a black woman.

677. She won three Grammys.

678. She wrote seven autobiographies.

679. She had a cameo in the 2006 film, Madea's Family Reunion.

680. In the 1993 film, Poetic Justice, the main character is a poet. The poems that he writes were actually written by Maya Angelou. The film starred legendary rapper, Tupac Shakur. Angelou was a fan of Tupac and called him "Six-Pack" due to his muscular physique. One day on set, Angelou saw Tupac getting into an argument with another man. Angelou diffused the quarrel when she walked up to Tupac and said, "When was the last time anyone told you how important you are? Did you know our people stood on auction blocks, were bought and sold so that you could stay alive today?" Tupac was so overcome with emotion, he burst into tears.

Michael Crichton

1942 - 2008

Written Work
The Andromeda Strain (1969)
Jurassic Park (1990)
Congo (1980)
Disclosure (1994)
The Lost World (1995)

681. John Michael Crichton is best known for writing Jurassic Park. Steven Spielberg bought the rights for the film adaptation before the book was even published.

682. Crichton was married five times.

683. Crichton believed that second-hand smoke doesn't cause cancer. He also believed that climate change is a myth. He even wrote a novel called State of Fear in 2005 where the characters learn the concept of global warming may have been invented as a scam.

684. He believed he had a dark entity (which he called a "tramp soul") inside his back which had to be exorcized. Through the exorcism, Crichton claimed that he saw the entity and said it looked like the demon, Czernabog, from the Disney film, Fantasia.

685. Many of his novels have been adapted into films including Congo, Rising Sun, Jurassic Park, The Terminal Man, Sphere, Timeline, and The Andromeda Strain.

686. He used to write under the pseudonym, Michael Douglas. When his novel, Disclosure, was adapted into a film, the main character was played by Michael Douglas.

687. In 2002, burglars broke into his house, tied him up, and robbed him at gunpoint. No one was harmed.

688. He was astoundingly tall, standing 6ft 9.

689. He has twice written about a futuristic amusement park where the attractions turn against the guests – Jurassic Park and Westworld. He directed the 1973 film of Westworld.

690. He died at the age of 66 from cancer.

Miguel de Cervantes

1547 - 1616

Written Work
Don Quixote (1605)

691.   Miguel de Cervantes y Saavedra was born in Madrid.

692.   Don Quixote was written in 1605 and is often seen as the first modern novel. Its original title translates into The Ingenious Nobeleman Don Quiojote of La Mancha. It revolves around a crazy Spaniard who goes on a journey to right wrongs in the name of chivalry.

693.   Many sources stated that all but two of Cervantes' plays have been lost. However, eight of his plays have been retrieved.

694.   He coined the term, "I've got bigger fish to fry" in Don Quixote.

695.   For Don Quixote's 400th anniversary, ten publishing houses released a version of the book. One publishing house sold 600,000 copies in a mere two months.

696.   He lost the use of his left hand when he was 34 during the Battle of Lepanto.

697.   There are 963 editions of Don Quixote and it has been translated into 25 languages.

698.   Although there have been a few film adaptations of Don Quixote, they have never turned out well. Terry Gilliam tried to adapt a film called The Man Who Killed

Don Quixote in 2000 but the production was met with disaster. The lead actor, Jean Rochefort, was considered far too old for the title role. Although Rochefort spent seven months learning English for the role, he left the production after he ruptured a disc. On the second day of filming, a flood washed away most of the equipment.

The disasters that befell the crew were documented into the 2002 film, Lost in La Mancha.

In 2017, Gilliam began production again with Jonathan Pryce playing the lead role. Production ended for the film on June 2017, and it is supposed to be released in 2018.

699. The last thing Cervantes wrote was The Travails of Persiles and Segismunda. It was published one year after Cervantes passed away at 68 from oedema. He believed it was his best work. Sadly, there is no official English translation of this story.

700. Don Quixote is the most successful novel ever written, selling over 500 million copies.

Miscellaneous

701. British author, Arthur C. Clarke, is best known for writing 2001: A Space Odyssey. He coined the word "Beep" in his novel, The Sands of Mars.

702. German poet, Friedrich Schiller, is most famous for writing William Tell. He kept rotten apples on his desk and said he couldn't work without the smell. His friends found the room's stench unbearable.

703. John Donne coined 342 words and phrases. He coined the phrases "No man is an island" and "For whom the bell tolls." Weirdly, he coined both phrases in the poem, Meditation 17.

704. Seven of Walt Whitman's siblings were named after American presidents.

705. Although John Keats is considered to be one of Britain's most influential writers, his work was only published four years before he died at the age of 25.

706. Robert Browning wrote the famous poem, The Pied Piper of Hamelin, in 1902. "Pied" means "multi-coloured" and references the piper's colourful outfit. Although this story has existed since the 1300s, most of these accounts have been destroyed and the 1902 version is considered the definitive one.
    In hindsight, Browning considered it a bad story.

707. William Wordsworth wrote the poem, I Wander Lonely as a Cloud, (which is often known as The Daffodils.) Wordsworth was born with anosmia, which means he was unable to smell.

708. The poet, William Blake, made most of his money from engraving rather than his poetry.

709. German playwright, Bertolt Brecht, was known for writing Life of Galileo, Mother Courage and Her Children, and The Caucasian Chalk Circle. He nearly hired a young Adolf Hitler to paint scenery for one his plays.

710. Rumi was a Persian born in 1207. He is the best-selling poet in America.

Nathaniel Hawthorne

1804 - 1864

Written Work
The Scarlet Letter (1850)
The House of Seven Gables (1851)

711. His surname was originally spelt "Hathorne." He added the "w" to disassociate himself from his great-great grandfather, Jon Hathorne, who was one of the judges who sentenced women to death during the Salem Witch Trials.

712. After he graduated from university, Hawthorne decided he wanted to become a writer. He spent about ten years in his attic, experimenting with his writing. He rarely left the attic and his sister, Ebe, brought him food and books as he worked.

713. He lived in the former home of the poet, Ralph Waldo Emerson.

714. Hawthorne published his first short story, Twice-Told Tales, in 1937. It didn't sell well and he was forced to make ends meet by working at a customs house weighing and gauging coal and salt.

715. The writer of Moby Dick, Herman Melville, was Hawthorne's neighbour.

716. His daughter, Rose, worked in New York with incurable cancer patients and was nominated for sainthood in 2003.

717. His masterpiece, The Scarlet Letter, was one of the first mass-produced books in America.

718. The Scarlet Letter sold out in ten days.

719. He was friends with the 14th US president, Franklin Pierce, and wrote Pierce's biography. Weirdly, it was Pierce who discovered Hawthorne's body when he died from gastrointestinal cancer.

720. Since Hawthorne was friends with the president, he had connections with the Democratic Party, which allowed Hawthorne to rub shoulders with many influential people in the political world. In the introduction for The Scarlet Letter, Hawthorne makes snarky comments about several politicians that he didn't like during his time with the Democratic Party. Readers bought the book to learn of the gossip in the political world that Hawthorne divulged in the introduction.

Oscar Wilde

1854 - 1900

Written Work
The Importance of Being Earnest (1895)
The Picture of Dorian Gray (1890)
Salome (1894)
An Ideal Husband (1895)
Lady Windermere's Fan (1892)

721. Oscar Fingal O' Flahertie Wilde's is often known as the wittiest writer who ever lived. His poetry and plays preached the necessity of style in life and art and would often attack Victorian narrow-mindedness.

722. He said that Edgar Allen Poe was "a lord of romance."

723. In 1884, he married Constance Lloyd. They had two boys, Cyril and Vyvyan.

724. Wilde had two half-sisters called Emily and Mary. They were the illegitimate children of Wilde's father, William. William did everything in his power to make sure their existence was kept secret and sent them to live with a relative in Monaghan in Ireland. That same year, they both died in a fire. It is unknown whether Wilde was aware of their existence.

725. Although The Portrait of Dorian Gray is seen as a masterpiece, it was torn apart by critics and was perceived as immoral and pornographic during his time.

726. Oscar Wilde is legendary for his witticisms. Some of his best quotes include –

i)   There is only one thing in the world worse than being talked about, and that is not being talked about.
ii) I can resist everything except temptation.
iii) We are all in the gutter, but some of us are looking at the stars.
iv) I have nothing to declare except my genius.
v)   The young are always ready to give to those who are older than themselves the full benefits of their inexperience.
vi) Some cause happiness wherever they go; others, whenever they go.
vii) A man cannot be too careful in the choice of his enemies.
viii) The public has an insatiable curiosity to know everything, except what is worth knowing.
ix) I love acting. It is so much more real than life.
x)   Dying is easy. Comedy is hard.

727. In 1895, he was caught having an affair with the son of the Marquis of Queensberry. Since homosexuality was outlawed during this time, he spent two years in jail for "gross indecency."

728. He was astonishingly tall, standing 6ft 3.

729. When he was released from prison, he moved to France and took on the name Sebastian Melmoth.

730. He spent his last few years penniless. He died from meningitis when he was only 46 years old.

Philip K. Dick

1928 - 1982

Written Work
Do Androids Dream of Electric Sheep? (1968)
A Scanner Darkly (1977)
The Man in the High Castle (1962)

731. Many of Philip Kindred Dick's stories were adapted into films including Blade Runner, A Scanner Darkly, The Adjustment Bureau, Total Recall, Next, and Paycheck. Although his work has been adapted by Hollywood more than almost any other writer, he despised Hollywood as he believed it represented a false reality. A recurring theme in all the films mentioned above is they revolve around a false reality.

732. Minority Report was supposed to be a sequel to Total Recall (which was originally called We Can Remember It for You Wholesale.)

733. In 1970, he wrote a book called Flow My Tears, the Policeman Said. Later in his life, he met a woman who had the same name as a character in the book. Not only that, she was the same age and her boyfriend had the same name as the character's boyfriend. The woman was involved in a crime ring and had an affair with a cop, just like the character.

734. Dick spent most of his life in poverty and made almost nothing from his books. Even when the films based on his work were successful, Dick made next to nothing since he didn't understand management or royalties.

735. He was divorced five times.

736. He had a twin sister called Jane who died when she was only two months old. Bizarrely, she died from an allergy to her mother's milk.

737. He sold almost a hundred short stories and about 25 novels during the 1950s and 1960s.

738. In 1974, Dick claimed that he was visited by a God-like entity which he called the Valis. This rattled Dick to his dying day and he constantly wrote about this experience in his journals. Later in his life, he believed the experience may have been caused by him developing schizophrenia.

739. The novel that inspired Blade Runner is called Do Androids Dream of Electric Sheep? He came up with the idea when he found a diary written by an Auschwitz Nazi Officer. It read "The screaming of children keeps me awake." Dick couldn't understand how a human being could perform unspeakable acts. He saw this Nazi as an automaton and then came up with the idea of how a machine would think if it believed it was human.

740. He died at the age of 53 from heart failure just before the film, Blade Runner, was released. He managed to see a 20-minute rough cut of some scenes. Although he was cynical about the production, he was impressed with what he saw.

RL Stine

1943 -

Written Work
Goosebumps Series (1992-1997)

741. Robert Lawrence Stine thinks of the title of his stories before he thinks of the plot.

742. Some sources state that nobody dies in the Goosebumps series. However, the villain dies in the second Goosebumps book, Say Cheese and Die! The main character of The Ghost Next Door dies in the first chapter.

743. It took him about three weeks to write each Goosebumps book.

744. When he was asked why he writes, Stine said, "I just like to scare kids."

745. When Stine was asked what he finds scary, he said, "The size of the universe."

746. In China, the Goosebumps title translates into "Chicken Skin."

747. His favorite Goosebumps monster is Jellyjam.

748. Although he's written over 430 books about ghosts, monsters, and aliens, he has no belief in the supernatural.

749. He has a phobia of swimming pools.

750. He has sold up to 400 million books.

Ray Bradbury

1920 - 2012

Written Work
Fahrenheit 451 (1953)
Something Wicked This Way Comes (1962)

751. Ray Bradbury was friends with Chuck Jones for over half a century. Jones created many Looney Tunes characters including Wile E. Coyote, Pepe Le Pew, Road Runner, Marvin the Martian, and many more.

    Bradbury was also good friends with Ray Harryhausen who was considered to be the best stop-motion animator of all time. Harryhausen worked on many movie monsters like the Kraken, Medusa, the Cyclops, the Hydra, etc.

    On top of that, Bradbury was friends with the creator of Star Trek, Gene Roddenberry and visited the set one day.

752. Fahrenheit 451 revolves around a dystopian future where all books are banned. It was banned in the United States.

753. Filmmaker, Michael Moore, appropriated the title, Fahrenheit 451, for his documentary, Fahrenheit 9/11, which revolves around the filmmaker's theory that the Bush Administration used the attacks on the World Trade Centre to push their agendas for war against the Middle East. Bradbury was unhappy that Moore appropriated the title of his book. Ironically, Bradbury did the same thing... twice. He took the title of George Orwell's book, 1984, for his novel, Beyond 1984, and Charles Dicken's A Tale of Two Cities for Another Tale of Two Cities.

754. He wrote Fahrenheit 451 on a rented typewriter in a library.

755. Fahrenheit 451 was supposed to be called The Fireman.

756. He didn't have enough money to go to college. After he finished high school, Bradbury visited the library three times a week. After ten years, he read every book in the library. He considered this to be the end of his higher education.

757. He was close friends with the director, Federico Fellini. When Fellini first met Bradbury, he said "My twin! My twin!" Bradbury was so fond of Fellini, that he grew to hate Halloween after Fellini died on October 31st 1993.

758. He never learned to drive and didn't fly until he was 61.

759. He is the great-great-great grandson of Mary Brady, who was tried for witchcraft in the Salem Witch Trails in 1692. Luckily, she was acquitted.

760. When he was asked what he thought of Fahrenheit 451, he said, "I wasn't trying to predict the future. I was trying to prevent it."

Raymond Chandler

1888 - 1959

Written Work
The Big Sleep (1939)
Black Mask (1933)

761. Raymond Chandler is considered to be one of the greatest detective writers ever. The most iconic character he created was the detective, Philip Marlowe. Marlowe appeared in many stories including Finger Man, The Big Sleep, The High Window, and The Long Goodbye. Marlowe was portrayed by Humphrey Bogart in the 1946 adaptation of The Big Sleep. He was portrayed by Elliot Gould in the 1973 film, The Long Goodbye.

762. Chandler encouraged Ian Fleming to continue writing his James Bond novels when Fleming wanted to quit.

763. Like many successful novelists, Chandler was asked to write several scripts for Hollywood. He wrote Double Indemnity, which was adapted into a film by Billy Wilder in 1944. Chandler collaborated on a screenplay for Strangers on a Train, which was adapted into a film by Alfred Hitchcock in 1951. Both films are now considered to be classics.

764. He was paid $10,000 for the screen rights to The Big Sleep. He was paid $2,500 a week to write the screenplay for Strangers on a Train. He worked on the script for five weeks.

765. He briefly quit writing at the age of 22 after his friend, Richard Middleton, committed suicide. Chandler

believed that if a talented writer like Middleton couldn't make it as a successful writer, he had no chance.

766. He was 50 years old when his first novel was published.

767. Chandler hated stories where an amateur detective could solve cases that stumped the police force by conveniently finding clues. He said these stories were unrealistic and it was like "having God sit in your lap."

768. His wife, Cissy, was 17 years older than him. Many people mistook her for Chandler's mother.

769. Bradbury was so devastated when his wife died, he tried to commit suicide.

770. He died from pneumonia at the age of 70.

Roald Dahl

1916 - 1990

Written Work
The BFG (1982)
Matilda (1988)
James and the Giant Peach (1961)
Charlie and the Chocolate Factory (1964)
The Twits (1980)
George's Marvellous Medicine (1981)
Fantastic Mr. Fox (1970)
The Witches (1983)

771. Roald Dahl used to be a British spy. His missions involved gathering information by seducing powerful American women. They were the best missions ever.

772. Originally, James and the Giant Peach was supposed to revolve around a gigantic cherry.

773. He wrote about his time at boarding school in his autobiography, Boy: Tales of Childhood. One of the most iconic moments in the book is when he and his friends were caned after putting a dead mouse inside a sweet jar in a sweet shop.

774. His first children's book, The Gremlins, was written in 1942. It sold so badly, many die-hard Dahl fans are oblivious to its existence. Weirdly, Dahl coined the word "gremlin" in this book.

775. In the early 20th century, Cadbury sent new chocolates to schools throughout the country for students to try. Dahl was one of the students who was sent chocolate and he obsessed about creating a new

type of chocolate to send to Cadbury. This obsession inspired him to write Charlie and the Chocolate Factory.

776. He married Patricia Neal in 1953. She starred in many films including Breakfast at Tiffany's and The Day the Earth Stood Still. She won an Oscar for her performance in Hud.

777. He stood 6ft 6.

778. Dahl briefly lost his sight after suffering an injury as an RAF fighter pilot in WWII.

779. His teachers thought Dahl was a dreadful writer. In his school report, his English teacher wrote, "I have never met anybody who so persistently writes words meaning the exact opposite to what is intended."

780. Dahl died from leukaemia in 1990. He was buried with his favourite chocolate.

Robert Frost

1874 - 1963

Written Work
A Boy's Will (1915)
North of Boston (1914)
The Road Not Taken (1916)

781.   Robert Lee Frost is often considered to be the greatest American poet of the 20th century.

782.   He won four Pulitzer Prizes for his poetry.

783.   Although his poem, War Thoughts at Home, was written in 1918, it wasn't published until 2006.

784.   In 1960, he was awarded the US Congressional Gold Medal. It is the highest award that a civilian can receive.

785.   Frost's life was filled with tragedy. Of his six children, only two of them lived beyond him. One child died from cholera at eight years old, one died during birth, one died at 28, and another at 38. Frost's wife, Elinor, died at 38 from breast cancer.

786.   Frost read the poem, The Gift Outright, at JFK's inauguration in 1961.

787.   He has many iconic quotes including –
i)   Good fences make good neighbours.
ii)   The reason worry kills more people than work is that more people worry than work.
iii)   The brain is a wonderful organ; it starts working the moment you get up in the morning and does not stop until you get to the office.

788. Frost is pictured on the 10¢ US stamp in 1974, which was the 100th anniversary of his birth.

789. Frost's most famous poem is The Road Not Taken. Most people think the title means one should "forge your own path rather than following the same path as everyone else." However, many readers misunderstand the poem. The second stanza states that both roads are "worn, really about the same." Frost believed that society desperately sought out meanings in insignificant incidents. He references this when he talked about his friend, Edward Thomas, by saying, "Whichever road he went, he would be sorry he didn't go the other."

790. He died at 88 years of age from a clot in the lungs.

Robert Louis Stevenson

1850 - 1894

Written Work
Strange Case of Dr Jekyll and Mr Hyde (1886)
Treasure Island (1883)

791.   He couldn't read until he was eight.

792.   Stevenson rewrote Strange Case of Dr. Jekyll and Mr. Hyde in three days after his wife burned the first draft. He wrote the 30,000-word novel during a cocaine binge.

793.   There is no "The" in the title, Strange Case of Dr Jekyll and Mr Hyde. Although this looks like a typo, Stevenson said it was intentional.

794.   He concocted the idea of Strange Case of Dr Jekyll and Mr Hyde from a dream.

795.   He had wooden teeth.

796.   He wrote a book called Kidnapped in 1886. A film called Kidnapped was released in 1960. This film is not related to Stevenson's book of the same. Weirdly, this film was directed by a man called Robert Stevenson.

797.   Stevenson invented the sleeping bag.

798.   He suffered from tuberculosis for most of his life.

799.   He moved to Samoa in 1889 and remained there for the rest of his life.

800.   He died from a cerebral haemorrhage when he was 44 years old.

Rudyard Kipling

1865 - 1936

Written Work
The Jungle Book (1894)

801. Joseph Rudyard Kipling was born in Bombay in British India.

802. Kipling wrote 39 stories before he was 22.

803. He wrote The Jungle Book in 1894. It was made up of three stories. Only one of these stories revolved around Mowgli. He wrote The Second Jungle Book the following year. It was made up of eight stories, five of which revolve around Mowgli. At the time of writing The Second Jungle Book, he was the highest paid writer in the world.

804. The Jungle Book is different from the Disney classic in many ways. In the original story, Baloo is grumpy, Bagheera is calm, and Kaa is friendly. King Louie doesn't appear in the book and was created for the film. Shere Kahn is killed by Mowgli after he forces a buffalo to stampede over the tiger while he sleeps. Mowgli then skins Kahn and dances around his corpse.

    Also, Mowgli's name is pronounced "MAU-glee," not "MOE-glee."

805. Kipling won the Nobel Prize for Literature in 1907. He was the first English recipient of the award since it was established in 1901.

806. He declined the Order of Merit, the Poet Laureateship, and a knighthood.

807.   Hindi was his first language.

808.   A French soldier was carrying Kipling's book, Kim, in his pocket when he was shot. Luckily, the bullet lodged itself in the book and he survived. When Kipling heard this story, he became friends with the soldier.

809.   Kipling was a huge fan of Mark Twain and went out of his way to meet Twain while he was in America.

810.   A newspaper incorrectly stated that Rudyard Kipling died on January 16th 1936. He contacted the publisher to confirm that he was alive. He died two days later.

Salman Rushdie

1947 -

Written Work
The Satanic Verses (1988)

811. Sir Ahmed Salman Rushdie was born in Bombay in British India.

812. In 1988, Rushdie wrote The Satanic Verses; a novel that some readers believe criticises Islam. As a result, Iran's Ayatollah, Ruhollah Khomeini, issued a fatwa; an order for Muslims to kill Rushdie. If anyone was even slightly connected to Rushdie, they were a target as well. The Japanese translator of the novel, Hitoshi Igarashi, was murdered outside his office. A mob set fire to a hotel to kill the Turkish translator, Aziz Nesin. Although Nesin escaped, 35 people died in the fire. The London bookstore, Collets and Dillons, was firebombed for carrying The Satanic Verses. Bombs were found in several Penguin bookshops. In 2010, Al-Qaeda put Rushdie's name on their hit-list. Although the fatwa against Rushdie is no longer in effect, it resulted in the death of countless innocents.

813. The Satanic Verses was banned in India, South Africa, Sri Lanka, Kenya, Pakistan, Sudan, Bangladesh, Thailand, Venezuela, Singapore, Indonesia, and Tanzania.

814. He wrote Haroun and the Sea of Stories for his son, Zafar, while he was in hiding. Rushdie couldn't meet Zafar during this time.

815. He went by the name Joseph Anton while he was in hiding.

816. Rushdie was knighted in 2007.

817. Rushdie worked at an ad agency after he graduated from Cambridge. He came up with several iconic phrases such as "That'll do nicely" for American Express. He also came up with the phrase, "naughty but nice" as an advertising slogan to sell cakes in Britain during the 1970s.

818. He's been divorced four times.

819. Although Rushdie is infamous for The Satanic Verses, he has written many children's books and other novels like Grimus, Midnight's Children, Shame, Fury, and The Enchantress of Florence. Although not all his books were successful, they were met with high praise.

820. When Rushdie was asked to comment on the fatwa, he said, "I wish I'd written a more offensive book."

Samuel Beckett

1906 - 1989

Written Work
Waiting for Godot (1953)
Endgame (1957)
Krapps' Last Tape (1958)

821. His play, Breath, is 30 seconds long. There is no dialogue or characters.

822. Samuel Beckett wrote a Buster Keaton short in 1965 called Film.

823. Beckett fought in the French Resistance during WWII. He was such an efficient soldier, the Nazis put a price on his head.

824. His play, Waiting for Godot, is nicknamed "The play where nothing happens" since two characters wait for a character called Godot who never shows up. Many people believe this is a metaphor for God since the name, Godot, sounds similar. However, Beckett wrote the play in French. "God" is "Dieu" in French and Beckett never considered Godot would be misidentified as God.

825. His most famous quote is, "Ever tried. Ever failed. No matter. Try again. Fail again. Fail better." It is used as a motivational quote by many schools and businesses. Richard Branson says he lives by this mantra.

826. A pimp stabbed Beckett in the lung in 1938.

827. His father died when Beckett was 27. Beckett was so devastated, he developed night terrors and depression.

828. He attended a lecture with renowned psychoanalyst, Carl Jung. In the class, Jung spoke about a girl who felt like she was never born. Beckett identified with this idea which may explain why his stories usually revolve around the emptiness of life, existentialism, and loneliness.

829. Beckett hated being in the spotlight so much, he refused to pick up his Nobel Prize.

830. While living in France, Beckett was neighbours with a boy called Andre Rene Roussimoff. Roussimoff suffered from gigantism and so, was too big to ride the bus to school. Since Beckett had a truck, he drove Rousimoff to school each morning and formed a friendship with him. Years later, Roussimoff became the wrestler, Andre the Giant.

Sophocles

497 BC – 406 BC

Written Work
Ajax (442 BC)
Antigone (441 BC)
Oedipus Rex (429 BC)
Electra (407 BC Approx.)
Philoctetes (409 BC)
The Women of Trachis (450 BC)
Oedipus at Colonus (401 BC)

831. Sophocles was an Ancient Greek poet and dramatist. He was taught by Aeschylus.

832. He entered 30 drama competitions and won 18.

833. He was considered the greatest writer in the world in his lifetime for 50 years. Ironically, his teacher, Aeschylus, was considered to be the world's greatest writer before Sophocles became a playwright. Throughout his career, he accumulated more writing awards than Aeschylus and Euripides combined.

834. He was bisexual.

835. Although Sophocles was a visionary writer, he didn't perform in most of his plays since he was a weak speaker.

836. He was a military commander, a priest, a politician, a treasurer, and a field general.

837. His play, Oedipus at Colonus, was performed posthumously.

838. He worshipped the God of Medicine, Asclepius.

839. Although he wrote 123 plays, only seven of them have survived. There are only fragments remaining of 90 of his plays.

840. It is unclear how Sophocles died. Different sources state that he died after he was bitten by a snake, choked on grapes, or dropped dead while reading Antigone aloud.

Stephen King

1947 -

Written Work
It (1986)
The Dark Tower (1998-2012)
The Shining (1977)
The Stand (1978)
Carrie (1974)
Under the Dome (2009)
Misery (1987)
Rita Hayworth and Shawshank Redemption (1982)

841. He used to be a janitor.

842. He is the most successful American writer in history.

843. King's first book was Carrie. He was writing it while battling depression and while under the influence of drink and drugs. At one point, he threw it in the trash, believing it was garbage. His wife, Tabitha, salvaged it and urged him to keep trying. It was published in 1974 and launched King's career. It was adapted into a film in 1976.

844. King coined the word "pie-hole" in the 1983 novel, Christine.

845. Stephen King didn't tell his children bedtime stories. Instead he made them tell him stories.

846. Stephen King was hit by a minivan driven by a man called Bryan Smith in 1999. The collision fractured his hip, broke four ribs, chipped eight parts of his spine, shattered his leg in nine places, and he required 30 stitches in his scalp.

When King regained his mobility, he bought the van and smashed it with a sledgehammer.

He then created a character called Bryan Smith in his Dark Tower series. This character drove the same minivan and nearly ran down a fictional version of King in the book. This character is described as an "irresponsible, mentally-deficient drug addict."

847. King's lawyers had to buy the van that hit him in 1999 to keep it from appearing on eBay.

848. King has the Guinness World Record for having the most movie adaptations of his work. He said the best films adapted from his books are The Shawshank Redemption, The Mist, and Stand by Me.

849. He directed the film adaptation of his book, Maximum Overdrive. In the story, machines come to life and start killing humans. In the beginning of the film, it is stated the machines came to life after being exposed to radiation from a passing comet. In the film's conclusion, it is stated that the machines were brought to life because of a UFO laser…. make up your mind, movie.

850. After King became successful, he was worried readers were buying his books simply because of his reputation. As a result, he wrote seven books under the pseudonym, Richard Bachman. These books were Rage, The Long Walk, Roadwork, The Running Man, Thinner, The Regulators, and Blaze. Although these books were well-received by critics, some were criticised for being too similar to Stephen King!

Sylvia Plath

1932 - 1963

Written Work
The Bell Jar (1963)
Colossus (1960)
Ariel (1965)

851. Sylvia Plath coined the word "dreamscape" in the 1958 poem, The Ghost's Leavetaking.

852. Her first poem, (simply called Poem,) was published when she was nine years old.

853. Plath's struggle with depression coined the term "the Sylvia Plath effect," which shows how common mental illnesses are among poets.

854. In the last months of her life, Plath wrote a journal. However, it was destroyed by her husband, Ted Hughes, after she died because Hughes didn't want his children to read about her battle with depression "particularly her last days."

855. Although she is known for her poetry, her novel, The Bell Jar, is considered to be a masterpiece. The 1963 semi-autobiographical book reveals a lot about Plath's battle with contemplating suicide. It wasn't published in the US until eight years after her death.

856. Her IQ was 166 according to a test she took in 1944.

857. Plath tried to take her own life many times. After her husband repeatedly cheated on her, Plath gassed herself to death in her London apartment while her children slept. She was only 30 years old.

858. Ted Hughes' mistress, Assia Wevill, moved into Plath's house. Sadly, she took her own life in 1969, only six years after Plath's suicide.

859. Plath's son, Nicholas Hughes, lost two maternal figures at a young age, which took a toll on his mind. He committed suicide in 2009. He was only 47.

860. Plath's editor, Al Alvarez, claimed that Plath and Hughes used black magic to enhance their poetry.
    Ted Hughes claimed to have used Ouija boards and read astrology with his wife. Plath told Hughes that she felt "feelings of jealousy and forces of witchcraft and black magic."

TS Eliot

1888 - 1965

Written Work
Murder in the Cathedral (1935)
The Waste Land (1922)
Old Possum's Book of Practical Cats (1939)
Four Quartets (1943)

861. Thomas Steans Eliot said William Butler Yeats was the greatest English poet of the 20th century and the biggest influence on his own writing.

862. Eliot won a Nobel Prize for literature in 1948.

863. Rum Tum Tugger is the most famous poem in Old Possum's Book of Practical Cats. It inspired the musical, Cats.

864. He had many nicknames including Deliberate Pedant, Old Possum, Aged Eagle, and Gus Krutch.

865. He was awarded the Presidential Medal of Freedom in 1964.

866. He coined two famous phrases, "The journey, not the arrival," and "This is the way the world ends, not with a bang but a whimper."

867. He won four Tony Awards.

868. He married Vivienne Haigh-Wood in 1915. They were together until she died in 1947. He then married Esme Valerie Fletcher in 1957. She was 38 years younger than him.

869. He died from emphysema at the age of 76.

870. Eliot didn't like Orwell's novel, Animal Farm, because he believed the author was too harsh on Joseph Stalin!!

Tennessee Williams

1911 - 1983

Written Work
The Glass Menagerie (1944)
A Streetcar Named Desire (1947)
Cat on a Hot Tin Roof (1955)

871. His real name was Thomas Lanier Williams III.

872. He was bullied maliciously by his father for being gay. His dad used to call him "Miss Nancy."

873. He suffered from paralysis between the ages of five and seven.

874. He won a Pulitzer Prize for his 1947 play, A Streetcar Named Desire, and his 1954 play, Cat on a Hot Tin Roof. Both plays were adapted into films and were met with high praise.

875. He battled depression for his entire adult life.

876. He used to work on a chicken ranch.

877. He was the head of the jury at the Cannes Film Festival in 1976.

878. When Williams was asked why he writes, he said, "Because I found life unsatisfactory."

879. Marlon Brando was his favorited actor. Brando played Stanley in A Streetcar Named Desire. Although Brando had a reputation for changing his lines, he said it was impossible with William's script because he

couldn't come up with anything better. Brando compared Williams' writing with Shakespeare's.

880.   He died at the age of 71 by choking on a bottle cap.

Terry Pratchett

1948 - 2015

Written Work
Discworld (1983-2015)
Good Omens (1990)

881. Terry Pratchett was incredibly loyal to his fan base and attended more book signings than almost any other author. Fans joke that there are more signed copies of his work than unsigned copies.
    Pratchett was known for his modesty. He once said, "I wouldn't pay more than a couple of quid to see me, and I'm me."

882. He used to work at a nuclear power plant.

883. Originally, Pratchett wanted to be an astronomer.

884. JK Rowling said she never considered the Harry Potter series to be a fantasy story until it was finished. When Pratchett heard this, he said, "I would have thought the wizards, witches, trolls, unicorns, and hidden worlds would have given her a clue."

885. His daughter, Rhianna, writers for video games including Mirrors Edge and the recent Tomb Raider reboot.

886. In 2008, Pratchett declared that he was suffering from a rare form of Alzheimer's called posterior cortical atrophy. Shortly after, he donated £500,000 for Alzheimer's research.

887. He was only 60 years old when he developed Alzheimer's. According to the NHS, he had to pay for his

Alzheimer's medication since he is too young to receive it for free.

888. He was knighted in 2009.

889. After his diagnosis, Pratchett became fascinated with euthanasia and presented a documentary about assisted suicide called Choosing to Die in 2011.

890. Pratchett was worried that someone else would finish his incomplete work after he died. At Pratchett's request, all his unpublished work was crushed by a steamroller after he died.

Tom Clancy

1947 - 2013

Written Work
The Hunt for Red October (1984)
Patriot Games (1987)
Clear and Present Danger (1989)
The Sum of All Fears (1991)

891. Thomas "Tom" Leo Clancy Jr. has a reputation for making his spy novels as authentic as possible. When his books are adapted for film, certain elements are tweaked... much to Clancy's annoyance. While he did the audio commentary of the film adaption for his book, The Sum of All Fears, he dismissed every single facet that wasn't 100% accurate. The director (who was sitting beside Clancy while he trashed the movie,) tried to explain to the author that certain scenes had to be changed to heighten tension. Nevertheless, Clancy pointed out the most minor flaws like how a satellite photograph's quality was too high, radar was too efficient, and the CIA weren't identifying geopolitical intel accurately.

892. He used to write a four-line paragraph for each chapter of his books and then had his co-author, James Patterson, write the rest. Although Patterson has practiced this technique for over two decades for many famous writers, he rarely gets any credit.

893. He has sold over 100 million copies of his books.

894. Because technology was limited in the 1980s, he had to save The Hunt for Red October on ten floppy discs.

895. He co-founded the video game company, Red Storm Entertainment, in 1996. As of 2017, it has made 35 video games including Far Cry 3 and Far Cry 4.

896. At his peak, Clancy was worth $190 million.

897. Clancy was 39 years old when he published his first book, The Hunt for Red October. He sold the rights to the book for $5,000.

898. His novel, The Cardinal of the Kremlin, was the most successful book of 1988. Clear and Present Danger was the most successful book of 1989.

899. The most iconic character that Clancy created was Jack Ryan. Although Ryan is usually depicted as a CIA agent in films, he eventually becomes the Director of the CIA, a National Security Advisor, the Vice President, and the President of the United States.

   Jack Ryan has been portrayed by Alec Baldwin in The Hunt for Red October, Harrison Ford in Patriot Games and Clear and Present Danger, Ben Affleck in The Sum of All Fears, Chris Pine in Jack Ryan: Shadow Recruit, and John Krasinski in Tom Clancy's Jack Ryan. Clancy said that he believes Ben Affleck gave the best performance of Ryan.

900. It is undisclosed what Clancy died from in 2013.

Toni Morrison

1931 -

Written Work
Beloved (1987)
Song of Solomon (1977)
The Bluest Eye (1970)

901. Her birth name is Chloe Anthony Wofford.

902. Morrison heard the story of a runaway slave called Margaret Garner who fled with her family from her slave-owner in 1856. When her family was tracked down, Garner was so terrified that her children would live as slaves, that she killed her youngest daughter. When she was tried for her crimes, Garner said, "I'd do it again." Toni Morrison found this story so harrowing, it inspired her to write her novel, Beloved.

903. Toni Morrison wrote an opera based on Margaret Garner's life.

904. She was a professor at Princeton University.

905. Her grandfather was a slave.

906. Morrison won a Nobel Prize in 1993. She is the first African American woman to receive the Nobel Prize for Literature.

907. Morrison read her own novel, Beloved, for the first time 30 years after writing it. She thinks that "it's really good!"

908. Beloved has been banned more than almost any other book in America due to being too intense for

teenage readers.

909. Morrison became traumatized after she lost her house in a fire. For years, she wouldn't speak to anyone unless they had suffered a similar loss.

910. Barack Obama awarded Morrison a Presidential Medal of Freedom in 2012.

Truman Capote

1924 - 1984

Written Work
Breakfast at Tiffany's (1958)
In Cold Blood (1966)

911. His birth name is Truman Streckfus Persons.

912. Capote was very superstitious. He refused to work on the 13th day of the month and skipped the 13th step of a staircase. He never left three cigarette butts in an ashtray and went berserk if he saw a hat on a bed.

913. Although Breakfast at Tiffany's is Capote's most famous book, In Cold Blood was considered his best and most influential novel.

914. He is a distant relative of the playwright, Tennessee Williams.

915. He was the inspiration for the character of Dill in Harper Lee's novel, To Kill a Mockingbird.

916. He produced 25 plays, two novels, 50 short stories, an autobiography, and over a hundred poems.

917. He looked very unintimidating since he was chubby, bespectacled, and stood only 5ft 3. However, he had a reputation for being an incredibly strong arm wrestler.

918. He is portrayed by Philip Seymour Hoffman in the 2004 film, Capote. Hoffman won an Oscar for the role. Capote was portrayed by Toby Jones in the film, Infamous, the following year.

919. Jack Dunphy was Capote's long-term lover. They were together until the day Capote died.

920. Capote's constant drug abuse caused him to develop liver disease, which led to his death at the age of 59.

Victor Hugo

1802 - 1885

Written Work
The Hunchback of Notre Dame (1831)
Les Miserables (1862)
The Man Who Laughs (1869)

921. Victor Marie Hugo was born in Doubs in France.

922. Although Hugo had many affairs, his most infamous mistress was Juliette Gauvain. They were together for 50 years. Hugo was sentenced for adultery in 1845 but received a royal pardon.

923. Hugo married Adele Fourcher in 1822 and had four children with her. Victor's brother, Eugene, was in love with Adele since they were children. When Adele married Victor, Eugene went mad and died in an asylum in 1837.

924. There are 48 different operas of Les Miserables. The Hunchback of Notre Dame (originally known as Notre Dame De Paris) has been adapted into 16 different operas.

925. Hugo's father was a general for Napoleon.

926. Just before he died, Hugo visited the construction of the Statue of Liberty. When he was asked what he thought of it, he said, "The idea, it is everything."

927. He claimed to have made love to his wife nine times on their wedding night.

928. It took Hugo 30 years to write Les Miserables.

929. Hugo took off all his clothes when he suffered writer's block.

930. Hugo wrote a novel called The Man Who Laughs which revolves around a man called Gwynplaine who was surgically disfigured so he has a permanent grin on his face. The story was adapted into a film in 1928. The character of Gwynplaine inspired a comic book writer, Bill Finger, to create the Joker in the Batman series. That's right. The guy who wrote Les Miserables and The Hunchback of Notre Dame is indirectly responsible for creating the Joker.

Virginia Woolf

1882 - 1941

Written Work
Mrs Dalloway (1925)
To the Lighthouse (1927)
The Waves (1931)

931. Her real name was Adeline Stephen.

932. Woolf's mother died when she was 13. Woolf's sister died two years after that. When Woolf's father died three years later, she suffered a nervous breakdown and was institutionalised.

933. She suffered from mood swings and bipolar throughout most of her life. She tried to commit suicide for the first time by jumping out of a window when she was 22.

934. Woolf was a British writer who was considered a pioneer in using stream of consciousness as a narrative device. This method helps show the constant thoughts and feelings that pass through the mind of a character. Although writers such as Edgar Allen Poe used stream of consciousness in their work and the term was coined ten years before Woolf started writing, it was Virginia Woolf who popularised the concept. James Joyce, Marcel Proust, and Irvine Welsh also use stream of consciousness in their writings.

935. Virginia Woolf loved writing. I don't mean she loved writing stories or poems. I mean she loved the act of writing. She practiced writing with different pens for hours at a time.

936. During one of her nervous breakdowns, Woolf believed the birds were chirping in Greek. This delusion lasted an entire summer.

937. During World War II, she and her husband, Leonard, were worried that the Nazis would emerge victorious. They decided to commit suicide by gassing themselves in their car if the Germans took over the country. They kept a large supply of petrol in their garage just in case.

938. The 1998 book, The Hours, won a Pulitzer Prize. It revolves around three women from different generations who were affected by Woolf's book, Mrs Dalloway. It was adapted into a film in 2002. Nicole Kidman played Woolf and won an Oscar for her performance.

939. She suffered from anorexia and called her body "monstrous."

940. Woolf didn't want her husband to witness another nervous breakdown so she committed suicide by filling her pockets with stones and walking into a river. The stones weighed her down and she drowned at the age of 59.

Vladimir Nabokov

1899 - 1977

Written Work
Lolita (1955)

941. Vladimir Nabokov was brought up in a very wealthy family in St. Petersburg. His grandfather was Justice Minister to the Czar, Alexander II. His father, Dmitri, was a Russian diplomat and Nabokov's mother, Elena, was the daughter of the wealthiest goldminer in the country.

When Nabokov's estate was confiscated by the Communist Party, his family were forced to move to London and then to Berlin.

Dmitri Nabokov was involved in a revolution in 1917. He was assassinated in Berlin in 1922 by a Russian fascist. Although Dmitri's killer was arrested, he was later released by Adolf Hitler. Vladimir Nabokov was worried that the killer would track him down so he fled to Paris.

942. Nabokov was trilingual from an early age and read Poe, Gogol, Chekhov, and Tolstoy throughout his childhood. He excelled in all his studies and performed well in soccer, tennis, and chess.

943. Lolita is his most successful and well-known work. Nabokov wrote sections of the story on cards. After several years, he believed the story was garbage and threw it in a fire. Luckily, his wife pulled the cards out of the blaze, saving most of them. Nabokov wrote with what cards were left and completed the classic novel.

944. He despised all forms of psychology and became enraged if anyone spoke about Freudism, Marxism, etc.

945. He had a vast butterfly collection. Later in his life, Nabokov donated the collection to Harvard University and the Zoology Museum in Switzerland.

946. His son, Dimitri, became an opera singer.

947. He taught at Harvard University in the 1940s.

948. He hated technology and never used a telephone or learned how to drive.

949. Nabokov suffered from synaesthesia which forces the senses (taste, touch, smell, hearing, seeing) to become linked. Because of this disorder, he claimed he could see and taste music.

950. Nabokov moved to Switzerland in 1960 and remained there for the last 17 years of his life.

Voltaire

1694 - 1778

Written Work
Candide (1759)
Plato's Dream (1756)
Oedipus (1718)

951. Voltaire's real name was Francois-Marie Arouet.

952. He spent a year in a French prison called the Bastille due to his controversial writing.

953. He was rumoured to drink 40 cups of coffee a day. Because of this, he could write for up to 18 hours daily. When he was too tired or ill to write, he dictated his stories from his bed to his secretary.

954. He cheated in the French National Lottery in 1729 to win half a million francs.

955. He wrote over 50 plays.

956. There's an urban legend that Isaac Newton discovered gravity after an apple landed on his head. This misconception was concocted by Voltaire.

957. He briefly served as a French spy for the Prussian monarch, Frederick the Great.

958. He was fluent in five languages.

959. Although Voltaire never married, he and his niece adopted a woman and referred to himself as her parent.

960. He died from uremia at the age of 74.

William S. Burroughs

1914 - 1997

Written Work
Naked Lunch (1959)
Junkie (1953)

961. William Seward Burroughs wrote Naked Lunch while consuming a morphine-based drug called Eukodol. Burroughs said he took Eukodol because he couldn't get any heroin.

962. In 1951, Burroughs tried to shoot a glass off the head of his wife, Joan Vollmer. He called it The William Tell act. Burroughs was so drunk, he missed the glass and shot Vollmer in the head, killing her. Naturally, he went to jail for murder. However, he only spent 13 days in prison since his family bribed the officers. He hid in Morocco for years to avoid the legal and social consequences of his actions.

   Bizarrely, he incorporated this murder in his book and film, Naked Lunch, and attributed his literal career to that incident. He told his friend, George Laughead, that to become successful, you need to "shoot the bitch and write a book. That's what I did."

963. He wrote a book called Blade Runner that has no affiliation with the 1982 film of the same name.

964. He started writing when he was 39.

965. He used firearms since he was eight years old.

966. He was good friends with Nirvana singer, Kurt Cobain. Cobain offered Burroughs the role of Jesus Christ in his music album, Heart-Shaped Box.

967. Burroughs wrote one of the first exposés on Scientology.

968. He co-wrote a book with Jack Kerouc called And the Hippos Were Boiled in Their Tanks. Although the book was finished in 1945, it wasn't published until 2008.

969. He was enlisted in the army in 1942 but was removed due to mental issues.

970. He died from a heart attack at the age of 83.

William Butler Yeats

1865 - 1939

Written Work
Sailing to Byzantium (1928)
The Tower (1928)

971. He was born in Dublin in Ireland. He is considered to be the most famous poet from Ireland.

972. Yeats was obsessed with the occult and mysticism. He even joined a secret society called the Golden Dawn that practised ritual magic. He joined a paranormal research team called The Ghost Club in 1911.

973. He helped form the Irish National Theatre Society in 1903. It is now known as the Abbey Theatre and it is the most famous theatre in Ireland.

974. He wrote 26 plays.

975. His brother, Jack, was the first Irish Olympic medallist. Jack won a silver medal for...painting. (This was when painting was in the Olympics.)

976. He was the first Irish person to be awarded the Nobel Prize in 1923.

977. He said the poet, William Blake, was a major inspiration on him for his own writing.

978. Cormac McCarthy named his novel, No Country for Old Men, after the first line of Yeats' poem, Sailing to Byzantium.

979. He allegedly declined a British knighthood in 1915.

980. He was in love with a suffragette called Maud Gonne for years and proposed to her repeatedly. When she rejected him for the fifth time, Yeats asked Gonne's daughter to marry him. She also declined.

William Golding

1911 - 1993

Written Work
Lord of the Flies (1954)

981.   William Golding's most famous novel is Lord of the Flies. It was rejected 21 times.

982.   Golding had a dream journal which he wrote in for 20 years. By the end of his life, it was made up of two million words.

983.   He received a knighthood in 1988.

984.   His nickname was Scruff.

985.   It took 40 years to convince Golding to allow Lord of the Flies to be adapted into a play.

986.   Lord of the Flies was nearly called Strangers From Within.

987.   He won a Nobel Prize for literature in 1983.

988.   He was incredibly sensitive to critiques on his novels. Sometimes, Golding left the country after publishing a book so he wouldn't have to read reviews of his work.

989.   Golding didn't enjoy how Lord of the Flies overshadowed his other work, which he believed to be superior.

990.   His novel, The Double Tongue, was published two years after Golding died.

William Shakespeare

1564 - 1616

Written Work
Hamlet (1599)
Othello (1603)
King Lear (1606)
Romeo and Juliet (1597)
Richard III (1592)
Macbeth (1606)

991. William Shakespeare married a 26-year-old woman called Anne Hathaway when he was 18.

992. William Shakespeare's name is an anagram of "Here was I like a Psalm."
    In Psalm 46 of the Bible, the 46th word is "shake." The 46th last word is "spear."
    Shakespeare was 46 when the St. James' Bible was completed.

993. In Shakespeare's early career, his theatre landlord grew frustrated as the Elizabethan author left quite a mess after his shows ran their course. When the landlord removed the famous playwright from the theatre, Shakespeare showed up with a gang, armed with swords and axes, and ripped the theatre apart. I don't mean they trashed the place. I mean they literally ripped the theatre apart and rebuilt it in a new place now known as The Globe. That's right. The most famous theatre in the world was built from stolen parts by a gang of thugs and thieves.

994. Six months after he married, Shakespeare's wife gave birth to his daughter, Susanna. Several years later, they had twins.

995.   There is no record of Shakespeare's life for seven years after his twins were born.

996.   He wrote the poems, Venus and Adonis in 1593 and The Rape of Lucrese in 1594. These were written while London was infested with the plague, which caused the theatres to close.

997.   William Shakespeare's plays were published as a collection seven years after he died.

998. It's common knowledge that female roles in the Elizabethan era were played by boys. But few people know that these actors were kidnapped, beaten, and forced to perform. You might find that bizarre. Why kidnap them? Why not pay them to act? Surely anyone young child would love the opportunity to perform in the country's most famous theatre.

   However, The Globe mainly attracted drunk peasants who were prone to getting very rowdy during a performance. Also, no one in their right mind would perform these scenes as the boys were expected to perform lewd and overly sexual acts.

   You might think this sounds a bit dubious. Queen Elizabeth watched these plays. There is no way she would allow this, right? Actually, these kidnappings were royally sanctioned. Elizabeth approved of this decision.

   However, Shakespeare was one of the few Elizabethan playwrights who didn't practice this. In fact, he mocked the concept in one scene in Hamlet.

999. The American poet, Ralph Waldo Emerson, loved Shakespeare so much that he believed that if aliens landed on Earth, they should rename the planet "Shakespeare."

1000.   Shakespeare invented hundreds of words such as –

Alligator, bump, Olympian, eyeball, puking, obscene, epileptic, addiction, assassination, bedazzled, belongings, luggage, dishearten, eventful, fashionable, ladybird, majestic, manager, inaudible, scuffle, swagger, laughable, uncomfortable, bloodstained, negotiate, outbreak, rant, marketable, savagery, jaded, dawn, grovel, torture, lonely, gnarled, mimic, unreal, and bubble.

He also invented the name, Jessica, in the play, The Merchant of Venice.

However, Shakespeare didn't invent these words from scratch. Many words were from different languages Shakespeare simply Anglo-Saxonized them.

Although he was the first person to use the word "assassination," the word is derived from the Arabic term, "Hashshashin."

Shakespeare invented many phrases including – Cold-blooded, hot-blooded, arch-villain, heart of gold, good riddance, full circle, the game is afoot, vanish into thin air, in a pickle, break the ice, off with his head, a sorry sight, wild goose chase, a piece of work, so-so, faint hearted, fight fire with fire, set your teeth on edge, seen better days, too much of a good thing, send him packing, wear your heart on your sleeve, laughing stock, what's done is done, baited breathe, not slept a wink, be all and end all, dead as a doornail, brave new world, out of the jaws of death, naked truth, lie low, love is blind, the world is my oyster, makes your hair stand on end, foul play, and fair play. He created over 2,000 phrases, which is more than anyone else has achieved in history.

Printed in Great Britain
by Amazon